To Be and Not To Be

To Be and
Not To Be

An Analysis of Jean-Paul Sartre's Ontology

by

Jacques Salvan

Detroit   Wayne State University Press   *1962*

To
Florence

*Bestriding the positive
solid reality to which it is
attached, this phantom
objectifies itself.*
HENRI BERGSON

Contents

Introduction

Existentialism is the philosophy of the Here and Now.

If, for a moment, as I reflect upon the fact of my existence, I refrain from considering myself as a man among other men, participating of the abstract character of mortal Man and sharing the essence of mortal Man, if I turn my attention to the actuality of my existence and come to wonder why I exist as a man, why I was born, let us say, at the turn of the century in a family of up-state New York Republicans belonging to the Episcopalian Church, why I am meditating here and now upon that fact, I can hardly fail to realize, probably with some sort of awe and wonder, that the question cannot be answered, that I just happen to have been born in such circumstances, that, in other words, my existence is entirely contingent.

Presently, as I become aware that I cannot account for my concrete existence, that there is no reason for it, at least none that I can relate to my awareness of it, it will strike me as being absurd. This awareness which I have of my existence in such or such a place, at such or such a time, seems merely to reflect a state of affairs which it cannot justify. This is what existentialist philosophers mean when they say *Existence precedes Essence*. I may try to dismiss this painful realization by considering myself from the outside, as others see me, as a human being among other human beings, as a link in the chain of life, as a person exercising certain social functions, as a person existing for others, and assume that in some way the justification of my existence lies in their consciousness. By so doing, I simply evade the question; my awareness of being the center of reference of my world will continue to reassert itself.

But if I reflect upon this awareness, it will no doubt appear to me as the ultimate and most anguishing problem, to be solved in solitude, and I will experience the feeling Pascal tried to convey by the celebrated sentence: "The eternal silence of these infinite spaces awes me."

This awe, this *anguish,* will be accompanied by an awareness of the necessity of *commitment,* since, after all, to quote Pascal again, I am "embarked" in this adventure of life without any directions, any sense of its meaning which might be grounded in the consciousness I have of my own existence. How could a mere reflection be made the basis of that which it merely reflects? In fact, how can this consciousness I have of my own existence be related to my existence, since it obviously is *not* my existence? No sooner do I reflect on the fact that I exist than I am seized with a curious feeling of not being that which I reflect upon. And yet, the necessity of justifying in some way that existence of mine is still with me. At once I have realized in *anguish* my *non-being,* and my *liberty,* together with the *contingency* and the *absurdity* of existence. Anguish, non-being and liberty are inseparable from the existential plane of thought. They generate a sense of guilt since, no matter what I do, I cannot find the justification of my existence in my awareness of it. There is a sense of guilt connected, not with some libido or Oedipus complex, but with existence itself.

While most of us recognize these data of the human situation for having experienced them at some time, few of us will seek in them the ultimate truth about our existence; the existentialists tell us that they give its true image and that any other viewpoint is an escape into inauthentic existence and a form of self-alienation. The average philosopher will reject the existential plane of thought as too subjective and too personal to provide a starting-point for the quest of the absolute or, for that matter, for any form of serious thinking. But the existentialist will claim that, through certain revealing moods, he is trying to define a human condition which is universal and of the utmost concern to everyone. When he says "I," which he does a great deal, he implies: "and you as well."

To that extent, existentialism *is* a philosophy, which moves on a plane generally reserved for religion, and embodies a certain attitude which those whom William James calls the "healthy-minded" may see no reason to adopt as more authentic than their own. There is, no doubt, an existentialist temperament and some critics have gone so far as to define the "existentialist man" as a distinct human type—an interesting but altogether unimportant discovery. The real question is why, at certain moments of history, the existentialist man's popularity singles him out as the representative man of his age. This has led to the common view that existentialism is a philosophy of crisis. This is true, no doubt, of the modern French and German schools and the case of Kierkegaard

xiii

might be considered as the exception that confirms the rule, since the Danish philosopher did not become popular until the times were ripe for him. The case of Pascal, however, testifies to the persistence, within the Christian religion, of a certain existentialist trend which may be traced back to Saint Augustine, who also influenced such independent thinkers as Luther, Calvin and Descartes. Emmanuel Mounier has pointed out that through Saint Augustine the existentialist tradition goes back to Plato. Indeed the debate which has been waged around existentialism was not merely between the Christian and the non-Christian views of life, but also, within Christianity, between the tradition of Saint Thomas and the tradition of Saint Augustine, between the Aristotelian and the Platonic trends. This would seem to involve a paradox since Platonism, in which the things of this world are considered as the shadows of immortal Ideas, or essences, appears, at first glance, to be the very antithesis of existentialism. The problem raised by this paradox cannot be examined here. Let us note, however, that, through Hegel, the Heraclitean philosophy of flux, the notion that there is nothing in this world which does not contain at once being and nonbeing, have also cast their shadow on a philosophy which was given at first as a reaction against Hegelianism, and that Kierkegaard perhaps, Heidegger and Sartre certainly, have brought back to the Augustinian tradition important elements of pre-Socratic thought.

Existentialism is then at once one of the few possible basic attitudes toward reality and a philosophy with a long tradition. It is better understood as the modern form of that tradition, which has never ceased to enrich and clarify itself while contending with other philosophical traditions.

As Augustine, bishop of Hippo, was writing his *Confes-*

sions and his *City of God,* the barbarians were invading his native North Africa and the ancient world was crumbling around him; the times could not have been more favorable for the birth of a philosophy of crisis. That philosophy was elaborated indeed in the anguish of the famous: *"Irrequietum est cor nostrum donec requiescat in Te":* "Restless is our heart until it may rest in Thee." The God that haunts human consciousness, like Sartre's absolute value, is of course more than a value; it is the most intimate part of myself: *intimior intimo meo* . . . , an absolute Thou, strictly the God of all religious existentialists. Reconsidered in the light of existentialism, Saint Augustine's is a most subjective philosophy which takes its point of departure in the fact that while I may doubt the ultimate reality of the world, I have to recognize that I exist as doubt, therefore as thought (Descartes' *cogito*); further, and this is of particular interest to us, that this consciousness of existing as a thinking self is always with me, even when my consciousness is completely absorbed by its object (Sartre's pre-reflective *cogito*). It is this *cogito,* situated in the Here and Now, which brings together the dispersed elements of reality and, in a way, creates the World (Heidegger's *Dasein*). Finally, the Augustinian notion of a fundamental guilt attached to existence itself is a basic element of modern existentialism, particularly in Heidegger and Sartre.

Descartes' merit was to break with the authority of the Aristotelian school and by returning, through methodical doubt, to the strict evidence of the *cogito:* "I think, therefore I am," to lay the basis of rational thinking as applied to the external world. Of course, he had only established his existence as a "thinking substance" and had to reach through the idea of perfection the existence of a God who would guarantee

that of the world around him. Nevertheless, having discon-
nected his thinking substance from the world of extension,
he could now proceed to translate extension into geometry,
algebra, and mathematics through the use of his coordinates.
He could also proceed to seek the liberty of mind within the
unity of a thinking substance divorced from extension. But
the hypothetical observer involved, as a center of reference,
by his coordinates, had little to do with the thinking self
which had produced the *cogito*.

It was up to Pascal to re-establish the *cogito* within the
Here and Now. Before thought can think itself as a pure
abstraction, it discovers itself in awe as the center of reference
determined by the existence of a body situated between the
two infinites of greatness and smallness, infinitely removed
from the beginning and the end of things which alone would
permit him to understand his situation, unable to understand
the absurd contingency of his existence here rather than there,
seeking in meaningless activities the diversion which will
permit him to forget his human condition, so miserable that
he could not be happy alone in a room, where he would have
to face that condition, so vain that it is enough for him to
push a billiard ball or chase a hare to forget it, guilty through
his very nature, which forces him to make his ego the center
of the world.

Yet, to Pascal, the misery of man is the sign of his greatness. The very fact that his existence appears to him contingent and absurd is a proof that there is in him an element
that is neither contingent nor absurd. His misery is that of a
dispossessed king. Alone of all the beings of creation, he
knows that he is going to die. While he is comprised among
them within the world, he comprises the world in some way
within his thought. The importance which he attaches to the

consideration of others, the fact that he wants to live an imaginary life in their minds, testifies to his recognition of the same element of infinity in them. It is no use for man to try to be either an angel or a beast; he is neither angel nor beast but an incomprehensible monster and the dogma of the Fall alone can explain that dual nature. This being recognized, the only rational thing to do is to take the leap into the irrationality of revelation. This brief outline does not do justice to the wealth of a thought from which none of the existentialist themes is missing, but it shows how, in opposition to Descartes, Pascal replaces the *cogito* within the Here and Now as a living center of reference.

Kierkegaard is to Hegel what Pascal is to Descartes. But Hegel in his turn can only be understood in relation to German romantic philosophy and its notion of *"Identität"*: identity of the self with the soul of the world, with the cosmos itself. Reflecting upon this notion, Hegel thought that some logic had to be introduced into this mysticism. The notion of *"Identität"* had to be corrected and rendered articulate through that of *"Negativität"*: I can consider myself as the ultimate product in the evolution of an absolute Being which has finally become conscious through me but my consciousness never coincides with what I am. As I reflect upon the present moment, it is already past. My life is in process of becoming. Hegel's philosophy is a logical elaboration of the old Heraclitean philosophy of change. Within the World Mind, Being generates its opposite Non-Being and the two combined produce Becoming. It must be that our finite minds are only parts of the World Mind actualizing itself. Being all parts of reality, the World Mind can mediate between them. Opposites participate in the same organic totality, and, in some way, they are the totality. Truth is Totality in the same way as the truth of the paragraph is the book itself.

Kierkegaard claims that one cannot adopt the viewpoint of the totality in this sort of objective idealism, because one would have to be completely outside of it to do so. Hegel appears to him as a self-appointed secretary of the absolute, living in a shack while building his metaphysical palace. The individual self is the real center of reference; truth is not totality, truth is subjective intensity and absolute belief in the absurd is better than lukewarm belief in the proven. In other words, Truth is Faith, a communication between the believer and God. God is not an object, a supreme Being, he is an *alter ego,* a Thou, an absolute subject. When we consider ourselves as part of a totality, we see ourselves as objects, and, to Kierkegaard, there is no objective truth. Each subjectivity is unique, closed upon itself, becoming itself through deeds, and martyrdom is the supreme message, because it awakens others to their subjectivity. The instant, which does not exist in Heraclitean time, is our chance to become free, the insertion of eternity within our becoming, our chance to make a choice before God and to answer every alternative with "yes" or "no." To choose is to choose oneself face to God. But, before God, one can only feel guilty: guilty of standing, finite and contingent, before the Infinite. Our finitude is our metaphysical sin and we experience it in various kinds of anguish. It is assumed in dread by the real Christian, who faces Jesus Christ as his contemporary, not once for all but in an act of faith constantly repeated. Of course, the average Christian is satisfied with mere conformity to the practices of his religion; but then he has no Self. Kierkegaard defines a hierarchy of three planes of existence, corresponding, it seems, to the beautiful, the good, and the true, and probably suggested by

Plato: the aesthetic plane, the ethical plane (which may be religious after a fashion), and the plane of faith which involves the acceptance of the scandal of God made man. One has to leap from one plane to the next but irony and humor may constitute between them two landings which constitute negations of the preceding plane. One should be careful not to remain there indefinitely.

Kierkegaard's call remained unheeded for a century for the trend was definitely toward scientific objectivity, and the very conception of free-will was completely discredited by serious thinkers. With Darwin, the romantic vision of a world in the process of becoming had turned into objective study of the effect of surroundings on living organisms. The reaction came in the late 19th Century with various forms of Idealism, but mostly through a new concept of evolution introduced by the prophets of life and intuition, with whom the prophet of the Superman may be loosely classified.

It is customary, in retracing the history of existentialism, to pass from the Kierkegaardian epigram to the Nietzschean rhapsody. Nietzsche borrowed from Schopenhauer his definition of the World as Will. The ultimate reality behind appearances, being-in-itself, was nothing else than the wild strife of life. Knowledge, abstract ideals, are only means to an end, which is power, and should be treated as such. God is dead, and Christian values appear to Nietzsche to be those of slave morality, the values of the herd and of democracy. The time has come for the Superman to arise and create a new table of values. The realization of the new liberty will come with anguish and nausea but it can be turned into joyous will. This is not a call to licentiousness: the Dionysian intoxication with life must be disciplined by the Apollonian sense of balance and harmony. But life must be accepted with the enthusiasm of the *amor fati,* for life repeats itself in eternal recurrence and our fundamental dilemma is to say "Yes" or "No" to life. It must be noted that Nietzsche's ideas had a considerable influence on the western world long before they came to be associated with those of modern existentialism.

The influence of Bergson and James, while not so well recognized to-day, was no less profound, in a less disquieting way. It is doubtful whether the philosophies of existence could have been born if they had not been preceded by Bergson's philosophy of life, and the latter is certainly due for a re-evaluation. Thanks to his scientific training, Bergson could meet the prophets of scientific determinism on their own ground. He discovered that *duration* did not play any part in scientific calculation, and that scientific time is really made up of simultaneities. Duration was the stuff of our psychic life, which consists in a constant interpenetration of all our "states of consciousness." Our whole past would always be with us if memory did not—paradoxically—screen from our consciousness whatever data are useless for action in a given situation. The reason why we cannot prove liberty is because the human intellect acts primarily through inorganic matter and can think only in terms of extension, multiplicity, exteriority and causation. On the biological plane, this means that with man, the vital upsurge (*l'élan vital*), of creative evolution took a very radical turn when it began to act through inorganic matter. Through this process, man managed to disconnect himself, to a certain extent, from the flux of life, retaining only as a sort of indistinct fringe, the intuitive privilege of direct intuition. This is his original sin. Only through intelligence can he formulate certain questions; only intuition could answer them. A closer contact with the world of intuition would free *homo faber* from his tendency to think of life, the mind, and duration in terms of inanimate matter and spatial time.

The resemblance of James' pragmatism to Bergson's vitalism is quite obvious, particularly in their formulation of the genesis of the free act. James goes further than Bergson in affirming that the truth of a statement is that it can be proved to work. Their critique of objective knowledge led both of them to the praise of the mystical fusion between subject and object which we find in James' *Varieties of Religious Experience* and in Bergson's *The Two Sources of Morality and Religion*. The last chapter of James' work might constitute an excellent introduction to existentialism on the psychological plane. Bergson's may elucidate the relation between religious and atheistic existentialism through his distinction between the god of the city, defined as the custodian of public morality, and the god of the mystic, defined as the spirit of creation recaptured through a sort of intuitive receptivity. It is not by mere chance that the publication of *The Two Sources* coincided with the new wave of mysticism sponsored by Romain Rolland, Aldous Huxley, and Somerset Maugham, and the triumph of the irrational in surrealism.

Meanwhile, as an implicit protest against the vogue of this new mysticism and the persistent popularity of naturalism, the philosophy of existence was born in Germany. As early as 1923, Martin Buber had defined its core in the three words: *I* and *Thou* and *It*. Buber distinguished between two planes of existence: the *I-Thou* and the *I-It* planes; the *I-Thou* plane is the plane of realization. The *Thou* may be God, the other, or the world. The *I-It* plane is the plane of orientation, or utilization, a plane of tools, on which we treat not only things, but others and even God as things; the *It,* indeed, is the original third person. The *I-Thou* and the *I-It* are structures; through the *Thou* a man becomes *I.* Buber's distinction between these two planes will remain valid in all forms of modern existentialism. We might add, at this point, to our definition of this movement that it is first and foremost a protest against objectification of the self and of the Other.

Karl Jaspers, whose philosophy appeared in 1932, distinguishes three planes of being. The *Dasein* (being-there) is the plane of objective and scientific knowledge as applied to the world and to man as an element of the world. *Existenz* concerns man as subject, i.e., as a being that *is* not, but *can* and *must* be, and transcends the world as *possibility* and *liberty.* *Transcendence* is the mysterious background of everything, neither the God of revelation, nor Descartes' perfect being, nor anything conceivable, because it cannot be the object of thought but can only be encountered in extreme, or limiting, situations. Each plane leads to failure, for reasons which cannot be developed here, and the rest is silence. Nevertheless, we realize ourselves, through that very failure, as we move from one plane to the next, and recognize that our sin is to be free and finite. Yet our liberty is the truth of our being, and what I want of the other, through whom I realize that I am myself, is his liberty. My relation with the other is therefore a love conflict.

The name of Gabriel Marcel is often linked with that of Jaspers, for reasons which are not completely obvious. They evolved their philosophy at about the same time, since Marcel's *Metaphysical Journal* was published in 1927, and his *Having and Being* in 1935. At first under the influence of

Bergson, he turned to existentialism, in fact invented the word, under the influence of Royce's concept of "fidelity," which detail ought to make us reconsider the accepted notion that existentialism is completely foreign to American philosophy. Like most existentialists, Marcel criticized Descartes for starting from the reflective moment when consciousness withdraws from life, and tried to replace the *cogito* within concrete existence—Within the Here and Now. When I say that something exists, I always connect it, no matter how indirectly, with my body. As in Pascal, my body is my center of reference, but as participation in the life of the world, rather than for contemplation. There is therefore no problem of the existence of the world; it belongs to the same structure as my body. But I may experience my participation on the two different planes of *Having* and *Being*.

Because my body permits me to act on things, I consider them as *objects* distinct from me. Those on which I can act without restriction, I consider as mine. My body appears to me as a tool which I have. So do other people, and for that matter, my own convictions, or the questions which I raise when I say that I *have* problems. Marcel's plane of *Having* corresponds to Buber's *I-It* plane.

To the plane of *Having,* Marcel opposes the plane of *Being*. Being is not a problem that I have, it is a mystery which I *am*. The *I* is not a "thinking substance," nor a succession of "states of consciousness," it is consciousness itself: commitment and fidelity. The self as fidelity is, of course, a mystery and the trouble with mysteries is that you cannot consider them without turning them into problems. Questioning this mystery of the self as fidelity, Marcel finds that it is basically commitment to that which transcends time; fidelity assumes the past, faces the present and builds up the future through continued

xxiii

creation. Joy is the feeling of inexhaustibility and is turned toward the future, while pleasure is connected with Having (to *have* a good time), which in some way is always related with the past. Between these two planes, we are placed in an alternative which forces us to choose between hope and despair. Like Buber, Marcel considers the *I* as always related to a *Thou*. God is the absolute *Thou,* and it is to Him that I am primarily committed. The god thought of in the third person is the god the atheist denies. "To thine own self be true" implies the recognition of some other Self. The *We* expresses that recognition. This, of course, raises the question of the *I* as a center of reference. Marcel, at this point, uses the Bergsonian distinction between open and closed religion and applies it to our relation to others. I am open to the other insofar as he ceases to form with myself a sort of circle inside of which I lodge him, or the idea of him.

The religious existentialisms we have considered so far insist on delineating the limits of the objective world but do not deny that it is a very real world. They protest against the objectification of the human person but stay clear of the pantheistic ideal of complete fusion with the world or with God, whom they consider as the absolute *Thou*.

With Nicolas Berdyaev, the outstanding member of the Paris personalist group, a Russian *émigré* who is also the prophet of Russian *émigrés,* the protest against objectification goes as far as to reject the objective world altogether, either as too remote from its transcendent source to have any reality, or as being the exclusive domain of the Prince of the World whose reign is singularly successful. His sources indeed are not only Kierkegaard and Bergson but also John, the Gnostics, the German mystics and German romantic philosophy.

To him, the material world, the world of physical laws and of necessity, this dead residue of a cooling divine fire tottering to its end, is largely an illusion of our consciousness. To the objectified world belong all moral and social laws, as well as the objectified figure of a God thirsting for power and domination. This God, created to the image of primitive man, is precisely the God denied by atheism. Atheism is like the dialectical cleansing of the idea of God, and is a necessary moment in the knowledge of the true God who is Spirit, Liberty and Love. This Spirit, in the cosmic process, has become conscious in the human person and has attained absolute embodiment in the man-God Jesus Christ. It can be found in any creative act leading to liberty and love. The person (as opposed to the Ego), shares with God a liberty which originates in the Non-Being anterior to Creation. The spirit of God is immanent in the person as the values of Liberty, Love, Truth, Justice and Beauty. It is present to evil, not as a judge but as an evaluating consciousness. It is preparing the new religion, which will be that of the kingdom of the spirit. It also leads to the end of the world and to the last judgment, which is the voice of God within conscience. What Berdyaev preaches is a direct and intimate union between the human spirit and the transcendent spirituality, the beginning and the end of all things, present in the world only in the form of a mystical human participation. It is difficult to condense the loosely related intuitive flashes which constitute Berdyaev's developments with the absolute certainty of remaining faithful to his thought. What seems to distinguish him from the other existentialists is a rejection of the objective world which recalls the Gnostics, and a metaphysical presentation of the apocalyptic vision so prevalent on the modern stage and in modern art.

Marcel and Berdyaev have, to a certain extent, clarified for us the relations between the religious and the atheistic kinds of existentialism. The latter, by reason of its method, is also defined as "phenomenological," which calls for a brief description of Husserl's "phenomenological reduction."

Edmund Husserl, born in 1859, is not an existentialist, but like most of them, he starts with a critique of Descartes' *cogito*. The *cogito* is valid, but Descartes should have said: *"cogito cogitatum"*: "I think whatever I think," for to be conscious is to be conscious of something, were it only, as in Descartes' case, consciousness itself. Consciousness aims at things and is primarily intentional; but Husserl had learnt from Kant that we know only phenomena, i.e., appearances. To study the various intentions of consciousness and establish a true science of the mind, Husserl goes back to that moment of universal and methodical doubt which precedes Descartes' *cogito,* and decides to stay there. To doubt is not to negate but to leave in suspense. This is what he calls "bracketing the world." The object is there only insofar as it is *other* than the subject. Husserl can now go about his business, which is to study the structures of consciousness, as securely as Descartes to his, which was the study of extension, when God had restored the world to him. By bracketing the world, Husserl is able to describe the intentionality of consciousness turned toward itself or toward the object. Perceiving, imagining, etc., are described as the intentions of consciousness.

The practice of this method, which excludes hypotheses and metaphysical speculation, may perhaps explain why Heidegger and Sartre seem to have access to a plane of immediate consciousness which is closed to us, although we recognize perfectly well the experiences described, once they have been pointed out to us. Both believe that since consciousness is mere empty intention, all one has to do to reach the truth of things is to let them be what they are, which is not as easy as it seems. Truth is not the adequation of the thing to the idea; truth is unveiling. Bergson had taught us that consciousness merely allows us to turn our attention from that which we do not need to know in order to act, which amounts somehow to the same thing. Consciousness is like a veil that we draw or withdraw at will. If we can be naïve enough, all we have to do is to retain a certain openness and the truth will appear as it is. There is no problem of knowledge; communication, no doubt, is something else. Fundamentally it is Being, the ultimate reality behind all the various modes of being, that Heidegger wants to reach, in his main work, *Sein und Zeit* (1927), but he thinks that this can only be done through a study of existential planes of being, which makes him an existentialist in spite of himself.

To simplify matters, we might consider successively the three planes of being which Heidegger discovers in his quest of Being: brute being (*das Seiende*), existence (*Ek-sistence*), and Pure Being (*Sein*).

Das Seiende is what simply is, the being of things: opaque, contingent, and absurd. As a present participle, *das Seiende* seems to indicate something in the process of becoming, but, since it is the present participle of *to be* used as a noun, a becoming which has become, perhaps something like Bergson's frozen life, or Berdyaev's cooling creation. Indeed it is made up of being and non-being. I shall refer to it as "brute being" rather than "brute existence," as is customary, to stress the very special meaning Heidegger attaches to the word *existence*.

Ek-sistence is reserved for man, or, as Heidegger prefers

to call him: "the human reality." It is an "ek-static" mode of being, which means that the human reality, as it tears itself away from the contingency of brute being, is always, in some way, beyond itself. It realizes itself in a triple movement of transcendence in space, in time, and toward others; or rather, it is this movement of transcendence which creates the World, Temporality, and Humanity. These movements of transcendence are not mere abstractions which in some way qualify existence; they are authentic existence as possibility. In authentic existence, I realize at once my non-being and the contingency of *what is*.

There is, however, an inauthentic as well as an authentic existence. In everyday life, I tend to identify myself with the impersonal abstraction which we call "one," "they," "people," and which Heidegger calls *"das Man."* I tend to think that I am in the world like any other being. I forget my possibilities in inauthentic time, which is merely a succession of "nows," and I skip from one to the other, or escape from the present into a future which is not *my* future because it is not my possibility. My relations with others are made up of small talk, equivocal attitudes, and the search for novelties. There is even an inauthentic conscience, which is the call of *"das Man"* within me.

I experience the inauthenticity of my existence through various revealing moods. A certain anxiety, inseparable from existence (*Sorge*) awakens me to my situation in the world as *being-there* (*Dasein*), cast in the world without reason, and I experience my dereliction (*Geworfenheit*). At the same time, man-made objects point to the task of organizing the world *with others* (*Mitsein*). Existence appears to me as a project which concerns me, or rather which I am. My being is outside of me, in the distance, in the future, with others. But my supreme possibility is death, which is already present to me as the possibility of there being no more possibilities for me, as my own impossibility, as a non-being. Between birth and death, my existence appears to me in its finitude, yet surrounded by an infinity of possibilities that I shall never realize, and for this sea of non-being which I cause to be, I feel a secret anguish which invites me to recognize myself guilty of having caused a lack of being. My finitude is my sin. Having accepted existing in finitude, I have to assume my guilt in resolved existence as *being-for-death*.

Being-for-death is authentic existence. I cannot give meaning to my birth, which is factual and contingent, but I can give sense to my death. My death is like the last note of the symphony, which rebounds on all the preceding notes, in which it was already present. It is not waiting for me outside, it is present in all moments of my existence as their supreme meaning. I am for death and Non-Being. As in Kierkegaardian repetition, I must experience this again and again to realize authentic temporality. Authentic temporality is not clock-time. Starting from the future, which is my project, it assumes the past and acts in the present as resolved existence.

Heidegger's quest of *Being* has led him only to describe various regions, or fields, of being. His originality consists in inflecting, so to speak, the verb *to be,* by making the preposition a part of it. Being-there, being-with, being-for, are not Being; these modes of being suggest a lack, the Non-Being which is the end and the meaning of existence. Heidegger's definition of Non-Being is one of his most startling contributions to existentialism and one which Sartre used to the utmost. Non-Being, of course, is not; Non-Being nihilates itself (*Das Nichts selbst nichtet*). It is therefore a sort of active force, and not an abstraction resulting from the negation of everything conceivable; it is negation which springs from Non-Being, and negation is only one of the various ways in which negative behavior expresses itself. Heidegger's unpursued quest of Being seems to have brought him closer to Non-Being than to Being. He lately has come to believe that perhaps they are the same, thereby drawing nearer to Hegel or, maybe, to the negative theology of German mysticism.

I should strictly have reserved for Jean-Paul Sartre the name of existentialist, which no other philosopher of existence, not even Marcel, who coined the word, seems anxious to share with him. Through Sartre, indeed, existentialism attained overnight a popularity paid for with much misunderstanding. This popularity was due largely to his novels and plays. Through these, he had endowed with a philosophy the "literature of commitment" which, since around 1930, was trying to evolve a new kind of humanism.

This literature had its roots in the French humanistic tradition of Montaigne and Pascal but it had also been influenced by the prophets of life and irrationalism. Nietzsche had proclaimed: "God is dead." Malraux answered "and so is Man." The new image of man had to be, not found in the image of God, but created by man himself with his flesh and blood, and the writer was to commit himself personally to this task. Malraux developed into a novel Pascal's parable of a group of prisoners waiting for death as the most fitting image of the human condition; but he made one of the prisoners rise above that condition by giving to two weaker fellow-prisoners the cyanide pellet which would have saved him from a horrible death. Saint-Exupéry's aviators seek a value that would transcend human life while they open the new trails that will establish the unity of *homo faber's* world. Camus depicts man as a stranger in a world of absurd contingency.

Sartre makes use of similar themes to illustrate his philosophy, but his novels, in my opinion, can only be fully understood in the light of that philosophy. If the reader understands Sartre's conception of man's fundamental project and of its variations, he will have no difficulty identifying the particular project represented by each character. He may even be able to identify, to a certain extent, the author's own individual project, for Sartre appears in his novels, sometimes in transparent guise, as Roquentin, for example, in *Nausea,* and as Mathieu in *The Age of Reason.* In Mathieu, we encounter a character who, early in life, discovered that his existence would be dedicated to liberty because he had just broken a precious vase. An obscure intuition had revealed liberty to him as negative behavior. Reaching the age of reason he was to discover the barren character of liberty for liberty's sake. But, as Sartre himself tells us, man can hardly know himself. Sartre's disciple, Simone de Beauvoir, allows us in her memoirs a glimpse at the tireless energy and intellectual honesty with which Sartre turned his negativity into constructivity in the slow and laborious elaboration of a coherent system.

Born in 1905, he had the advantage of finding in the literature of commitment and in the works of his predecessors most of the elements of the system he wanted to create. As a student of philosophy at the *École Normale Supérieure,* he could apply his critical sense against any system tending toward self-delusion or objectification on the subjective plane. His drawings of imaginary metaphysical animals showed that he had already reached that stage of self-satisfied negativity, which Kierkegaard sees in humor, and which, according to him, may precede the leap to the irrational. At the same time, Simone de Beauvoir tells us, he disliked society but did not dislike disliking it. As a professor in provincial *lycées,* he had a difficult time fitting himself into the academic hierarchy. At the French Institute in Berlin, where he had been sent on a scholarship to study Husserl, it was a great relief for him to be able to recapture the liberty of student life and forget adult responsibility. Back in France, and already applying Husserl's methods to various works, he was for a while disturbed in his intellectual detachment by the Spanish Civil War, but it was not until the Second World War, while serving in the Army Weather Service near Strasbourg, that a sense of responsibility toward the next generation dawned upon him, together with the conception of a system of ethics consisting in "assuming situations" and surpassing them in action. The few months he spent in a prison camp confirmed him in this resolution. Repatriated in 1941, he resumed his teaching in Paris *lycées* for a while, then resigned to dedicate himself to writing and political activities. The times were only too favorable for a literature of crisis. The "extreme situations" imagined by Jaspers had become daily realities. Sartre has described them in an often quoted passage of *The Republic of Silence:*

Exile, captivity, and especially death (which we usually shrink from facing at all in happier days) became for us the habitual objects of our concern. We learnt that they were neither inevitable accidents, nor even constant and inevitable dangers, but that they must be considered as our lot itself, our destiny, the profound source of our reality as men. At every instant we lived up to the full sense of this commonplace little phrase: "Man is mortal!" And the choice that each of us made of his life was an authentic choice because it was made face to face with death, because it could always have been expressed in these terms: "Rather death than. . . ." And here I am not speaking of the élite among us who were real Resistants, but of all Frenchmen who, at every hour of night and day throughout four years answered NO. . . . All those among us . . . who knew any details concerning the Resistance asked themselves anxiously "If they torture me, shall I be able to keep silent?"

Thus the basic question of liberty was posed, and we were brought to the verge of the deepest knowledge that man can have of himself. For the *secret of man* is not his Oedipus complex or his inferiority complex: *it is the limit of his own liberty, his capacity for resisting torture and death.*[1]

This passage clearly reveals, in Heideggerian terms, how definitely liberty was associated in his mind with negation. It is this close association which permitted him to write the sentence which puzzled so many of his readers: "We were never so free as under the occupation." A trick of fate had allowed him to live his negativity on the plane of heroism. Saying "no" to evil was not mere rhetoric with him, for he could manage, so Simone de Beauvoir tells us, to discover "a core of non-being" in the acute suffering of the most severe illness. Unfortunately, if he was singularly successful in his affirmation of human liberty through negativity, both in his life and in his works, he was less so in his constructive political program. His first group, "Socialism and Liberty" found few sponsors, his "Rally for Revolutionary Democracy" had few adherents. Fewer still are those who are willing to follow him in his recent attempts to reform Marxism from inside while modestly claiming that his existentialism is merely an ideology derived from Marx. Many of his admirers will no doubt feel that, in regard to a system which he once pursued with his sarcasm, the philosopher is entirely too respectful.

Sartre has been called the philosopher of negativity and it is as such, in my opinion, that he made his greatest contribution to philosophy. He succeeded in formulating an epistemology. If he did not manage to do away with the mystery of Being, he offered a solution to the most irritating problem of knowing. His definition of knowledge as "identity denied" should be welcome by those who are satisfied neither by "objective knowledge" nor by "mystical intuition." In this respect, his philosophy of existence marks a progress on the philosophy of Life. Bergson's phantom of Non-Being, striding the solid positive reality to which it is attached, is a very real phantom, since while the solid positive reality could be without him, he still manages to ride and govern it.

It is as the philosopher of negativity that Sartre should be studied.[2] The concept of negativity, made articulate by Hegel on the plane of the absolute, stretched like a bridge between Heaven and earth in Berdyaev's mystical vision, made active on the plane of existence by Heidegger, is the very basis of Sartre's system. Sartre starts where Heidegger ends, with the discovery of a nihilating Non-Being. I prefer to translate Sartre's *néant* as non-being, rather than nothingness, so as to preserve a present participle that may suggest in some way this nihilating action. As early as 1936, Sartre had identified this nihilating non-being with the pre-reflective *cogito* in his essay: *La Transcendance de l'ego*. In *The Emotions* (1939), he studied the relations of this pre-reflective *cogito* with the world, and tried to prove that emotions do not determine our actions but constitute a certain way in which we choose to live these relations. In *The Psychology of the Imagination* (1940), he rejected the conception of images as faded perceptions, stored in the mind like discolored photographs in the family album, to establish the theory that imagination is merely consciousness aiming at an absent or non-existent object on the background of a non-existent world.

In *Being and Nothingness* (*L'Être et le néant*, 1943), detailed presentation of which is the object of this book, Sartre starts by establishing the presence of a pre-reflective *cogito* in the very act of perception. He defines this primary consciousness as simply *not being* the object, and as *being-for-itself*. The object of perception is defined as *being-in-itself*, identical with itself, in fact as *being* itself.

Sartre proceeds with the analysis of consciousness as being-for-itself. Questioning the being of the for-itself, he derives, in Cartesian fashion, the answer from the question. Questioning involves the possibility of a negation, and negation the possibility of a non-being. Sartre tries to prove that negation derives from non-being, which is already in the heart of being. Consciousness is the irruption of non-being into the positive world. Consciousness, then, is an absolute non-being, which negates its identity with the world, itself, and other consciousnesses. These three forms of negation constitute what Sartre calls the three *"eḳ-stasies"* of the for-itself.

The first *eḳ-stasy* is that of the in-itself modifying itself into the for-itself by secreting its own non-being. The reader should note that, from an absolute non-being, consciousness turns into a qualified non-being by isolating the "this" or the "that" from its background through external negation, but negates at the same time its identity with the "this" or "that." As in Bergson and Heidegger, the world appears as a tool-complex, and consciousness as an absolute center of reference for its organization. The non-being of consciousness is the source of its liberty inasmuch as it breaks the chain of causality. Liberty is directly experienced in anguish; we may experience it before a past to be assumed or before the future as possibility. Temporality is also an *ek-static* structure through which the for-itself, as a mere presence to that which it is not, negates its in-itself which becomes the past, and projects itself as a future presence to that which is not yet in existence. We run away from liberty in such self-objectifications as determinism, the spirit of seriousness, psychologism, Bergsonism, and bad faith generally. Bad faith consists in trying to objectify the various movements of the for-itself as if they had an existence of their own. Bad faith, as a possibility, throws light on the reflective process.

Reflection is the second *ek-stasy* of the for-itself. In its purified form, the for-itself would have to admit its non-being, its liberty and its transcendence; it would have to assume the total situation in the light of its project, and would not be very different from Heidegger's resolved existence. Most of the time, it appears as an attempt to consider the various movements of the for-itself as if they were in themselves, with a life of their own. It is the basis of psychology and, to a great extent it is an attempt to see ourselves as others see us. Since our primary consciousness and our reflective consciousness are really one, it is a precarious plane of being which already implies *being-for-others.*

Being-for-others is the third *ek-stasy* of consciousness. Since any attempt to become an object for myself is bound to fail, I may try to be at once object and subject for the Other. As I discover my objectivity for him (as transcended-transcendence) in his glance, I may be tempted to retain it by becoming for him a limiting, or fascinating, object, with the ultimate end of forcing him to recognize me also as subject. The realization of this project is made precarious by the fact that, if I become a subject for him, the Other in his turn will become for me an object eager for my recognition of his subjectivity.

Its failure may lead to masochism, which is the definite adoption of our objectivity for others. This line of behavior is the source of love, and also of language, inasmuch as language is a form of seduction. Another line of behavior toward the Other consists in affirming my subjectivity by treating him as an object; it may take the form of indifference, sex, or, in extreme cases, of sadism, and is also bound to fail. The compromise generally adopted in such a difficult situation is to accept the limitations imposed upon us by the subjectivity of others without renouncing our own (I reject myself-rejected), or to adopt the impersonal existence of the interchangeable human being described by Heidegger as *"das Man."* The same relations prevail in regard to collectivities; the object pronoun *us* expresses the common objectivity of those who feel they are being used or dominated by another group or by an individual. As fascism, it may turn into collective masochism. It is, however, the original sense of collective existence. The subject form *we* refers to the assumption of a common subjectivity but only in protest against common objectification. The masters consider themselves, not as a class but as individuals. There is, for Sartre, no "togetherness" on the plane of being. My consciousness appears to me as an absolute center of reference in which others figure as objects. I either have to treat the other as an object within my world, or figure as an object in his, thereby degrading either him or myself, and this is the source of existential guilt and of the original sin. The only authentic *Mitsein* is the common subjectivity assumed by several individuals facing the same object in a common endeavor: in other words, the team spirit.

Liberty tends toward the realization of an absolute value which is being-in-itself-for-itself. As a lack of being, the for-itself craves to ground being in its transparency and in its liberty. All human activities can be reduced to this fundamental project: we basically make things to have them; having is an extension of my being, inasmuch as I can act on the thing possessed or destroy it. In politics, I either try to retain the world I have made mine, or to be the origin of a new world. Within this fundamental human project, there are many variations which constitute individual projects. It is difficult for me to know what my individual project is, because I am that project. It could be discovered by existential psychoanalysis through my reactions to the qualities of things. While these have the same *meaning* for all, they may be values or *anti-values* for us. Appropriation of things, or of the qualities of things, can only take place on a symbolic plane. The ideal value of being-in-itself-for-itself, which corresponds to the notion of God, cannot be realized. As the being who wants to be God, man is a useless passion.

Sartre has been called a romantic rationalist,[3] and rightly so, insofar as his philosophy of negativity is that of Hegel transferred to the plane of the *cogito*. He has called himself, and he has been called, a humanist,[4] and with good reasons. While he does not believe in a human "nature," the French humanistic conception of a "human condition," which is the same for all, confers upon his judgments a certain universality, and provides him with a general background for his study of the structures of consciousness. While he does not believe in psychology, his descriptions of various patterns of behavior are of prodigious interest to the reader. Whether the reader uses the criteria of coherence or of workability, he cannot fail to find in them a great deal of truth and of novelty. The humanistic character of Sartre's existentialism is, for most readers, its most interesting feature and its greatest weakness.

Sartre's humanism severs man at once from the world of elementary life and from the metaphysical world. Of course, this is the unavoidable result of a phenomenological method which merely claims to describe existential modes of being. The trouble is that this method cannot function without some hypotheses concerning the ultimate nature of being-in-itself. Sartre hesitates between being-in-itself as known: compact, opaque and identical with itself, in fact Being itself, and a being-in-itself posited by an as-if philosophy as already containing non-being, coiled in its core like a worm. Sartre's Being, already full of holes, is, to start with, a synthesis of Being and Non-Being, which involves a Hegelian, or Bergsonian, presupposition. The confusion may be due in part in the difficulty of retaining in French Heidegger's distinction between *das Seiende* and *Sein,* but only in part, for Sartre dismisses the world of life together with the world of things, as merely persisting in being, without any regard for whatever suggestions might be offered by the spectacle of the striving toward indeterminancy implied in the evolution of species.

In the same way, Sartre dismisses the transcendental world by placing his transcendence within immanence. Yet, again, in order to explain movement, he has to have recourse to the Heraclitean postulate that movement is a "lesser being," and, in order to explain the structure of being-for-others as "detotalized totality," to postulate, on the metaphysical plane, a Hegelian totality of mind. This brings us to the question of his well-known atheism.

Sartre's existentialism has been called postulatory atheism,[5] altogether wrongly, as should be obvious by now. There is nothing postulatory about his atheism in *L'Être et le néant.* He would not deny the possibility of a divine subjectivity fused with the world. The God whom Sartre denies is the same objectified and separate third person God whom all religious existentialists reject; but the singular aggressivity of his personal feud with that God had led some critics to think that the philosopher protested too much, and to interpret his protest either as implicit recognition leading to conversion, or as diabolical perversity. Sartre does not deny the possibility of establishing a system of metaphysics which would investigate Being from the data of his ontology but he does not in any way suggest its desirability. Yet, such a system might help to formulate the ethics of liberty which he promised but never completed.

All in all, the limitations which we have made bold to point out in Sartre's system are due to the very negativity which is the source of his greatness insofar as this negativity is compatible with the passionate intellectual detachment whose ultimate aim is to unveil the truth. On the humanistic plane which extends between the world of Life and the world of metaphysics, he has managed to give us a freer access to the structures of our consciousness. Even if one finds that his for-itself is rather active, as an absolute non-being, for all the operations it has to perform, one still has to admit that his descriptions throw much light on the mystery of knowledge. We must accept Sartre for what he has to offer, and what he has to offer is a great deal, as psychoanalysts and even theologians have found out. He will no more convert believers to his atheism than Pascal converted atheists to Christianity, but may help them and for that matter, all his readers, to see more clearly into themselves. When we consider that Sartre fits into a coherent and original system elements from Descartes, Spinoza, Hegel, Kierkegaard, Nietzsche, Bergson, Jaspers, Heidegger of course, the Gestaltists, Freudian psychoanalysis, and even behaviorism, not to mention a wealth of concrete personal experience, we may well wonder whether that system does not constitute a sort of modern "sum" of whatever philosophical knowledge is consistent with the existential outlook on the humanistic plane. It is, to say the least, an imposing structure, and one that deserves to be rendered more accessible to the fairly wide English-speaking public still interested in answering the challenge of existentialism.

The present work was undertaken, and its first draft completed, before the publication of Hazel Barnes' translation, (*Being and Nothingness*) at a time when the public had no access to Sartre's philosophy other than through a few superficial, erroneous, prejudiced, or incomplete reviews, technical accounts incomprehensible to the layman, or the sort of vulgarization that does away with philosophical problems by ignoring them. Since then, many studies have come out which, even when fundamentally adverse, have managed to maintain a high level of intellectual honesty. Full justification for the present work no longer lies in the fact that it fulfils a recognized need, but in the somewhat different way in which it fulfils that need.

My presentation aims at allowing the reader to follow Sartre's thought on three levels. The lines in italics indicate the sequence of arguments on the philosophical plane. The text embodies the development of these arguments on a somewhat more familiar plane of thought, and supplies their concrete illustration, either directly borrowed from Sartre, or boldly supplemented by me. Furthermore, since we are dealing with a sort of descriptive ontology, it seemed to me that the reader might find it a little easier to follow a development in which the very concept of *being* would figure as a sort of guiding line. I, therefore, slightly modified the headings of *L'Être et le néant,* to conform to a general scheme which,

I believe, accords with the fundamental structure of that work. As M. Sartre told me, when I submitted to him the project of this study, there is no definitive formulation of ideas. My presentation, through somewhat modified headings, addition of concrete examples, and the use of a vocabulary intended less, at times, for rigorous demonstrations than for the communication of an intention, was undertaken in good faith to help the reader share with me the profit which I believe I have derived from the wealth of Sartre's thought.

This work, therefore, is expository rather than critical. In another book, I intend to present a study of Sartre's literary treatment of certain themes, and to attempt to situate existentialism further in modern thought by examining its relations to humanism, vitalism, and mysticism.

Mr. Everett Knight, formerly of Glasgow University, was kind enough to read my manuscript and offer suggestions as to the best English rendering of some ideas; to him, to Professor Henri Peyre for his most precious encouragement, and to Ita Kanter for many suggestions concerning the present edition, the author's thanks are due.

J. S.

I Being-In-Itself

1. To be is to be perceived.

The phenomenal world consists in many series of connected appearances.

Perhaps the most helpful statement one can make in the way of introducing existentialist philosophy is that it is a manner of thinking which tries to account at once for the observer and for the world observed. In this, existentialism accomplishes in philosophy a reform similar to that accomplished in science through the theory of relativity. For the existentialist philosopher as for the modern scientist, no reality can be known except within the frame of reference determined by the existence of the observer. To the observer, the world is made up of series of connected appearances.

Yet the totality of possible appearances within each series is inexhaustible; it constitutes the essence of the object.

1

Let us notice, however, that each appearance points to other appearances within a series. The chair may appear to me, the observer, in a certain perspective, but the particular aspect which the chair assumes in that perspective refers to innumerable other aspects of the chair, or reappearances of the same aspect. We may do away with the notion that there is an inside and an outside of reality, a noumenon hiding behind a phenomenon, but we have to replace that opposition by the opposition between the finitude of a single appearance and the infinity of possible appearances within the same series. It is to that series of all the possible appearances of the object that I refer when I speak of the idea or of the essence of that object.

It points to the objectivity of the phenomenon, outside of consciousness, but the being of the phenomenon *remains distinct from the* phenomenon of being. *Yet, the being of the phenomenon demands the transphenomenality of being, which appears to consciousness as the phenomenon of being.*

This essence does not constitute the ultimate reality of the object, as do Platonic Ideas. About the reality of the object, I know nothing. I can only be sure of its objectivity: it is outside of my consciousness and I am not the object. The object still is a connected series of appearances. But how can that which merely appears be said to be? What do I mean when I say that reality is appearance? What is the being of appearance, the being of the phenomenon? When I try to think, for instance, of the ultimate reality of the chair, of its being, is it the being of the chair which now appears to me? Not at all. I cannot question myself about the being of the chair without passing to the idea of being in general and forgetting the

2

chair. Being as such, being per se, appears to me, not the being of the chair. Somehow, then, the appearance of the object—which is the being of the phenomenon—refers to being per se, which appears to me as the phenomenon of being, yet is not identical with the being of the phenomenon. The chair *is* because I perceive it. It seems as if I, as perceiver, conferred being upon the chair. Does this mean that, as Berkeley claims, to be is to be perceived?

2. To be is to be perceived by a perceiver who is: the pre-reflective *cogito*.

Being per se would seem to be conferred by consciousness, which is "the transphenomenal dimension of being of the subject." [1]

Like most existentialists, Sartre believes that being is revealed to us directly in such experiences as ennui, nausea, etc. As distinguished from knowledge of being—the ontological proof—such experiences are known as "ontic revelations." Could this being, which I experience directly, and which appears to consciousness as the phenomenon of being, be the foundation required by the appearance of the object? Could this foundation be merely the consciousness of the subject? Is it true that *esse est percipi,* that to be is to be perceived?

Consciousness is as intention. It has no contents and merely aims at things.

In a way yes, but not because consciousness *knows* the object and knows itself at the same time; in that case we would have to explain what knowledge *is*. The being of knowledge must be established before the knowledge of being. The object perceived must, as appearance, be perceived by a perceiver who *is*. This perceiver is consciousness not inasmuch as it knows but inasmuch as it *is*. What is the being of consciousness? Consciousness is intention. Every consciousness, as Husserl showed and as introspection will confirm, is consciousness of something. Consciousness has no contents, it merely aims at things. "A table is not *in* consciousness, even as a representation." [2]

Yet, *"every positional consciousness of an object is at the same time non-positional consciousness of itself."* [3]

Consciousness is intention but at the same time it is consciousness of self. It exists by itself: "the necessary and sufficient condition for a knowing consciousness to be knowledge *of* its object is that it be conscious of itself as being that consciousness":

> It is a necessary condition: If my consciousness were not conscious of being consciousness of the table, it would then be consciousness of that table without having any consciousness of being so . . . , an unconscious consciousness—which is absurd. This is a sufficient condition: it is enough for me to be conscious of having consciousness of that table for me to have in fact this consciousness. It certainly does not permit to affirm that that table exists *in itself*—but that it exists for me. [4]

In other words, I cannot be conscious of the table in front of me without being simultaneously conscious of the fact that I am not the table. This is what led philosophers to say that in the act of perception I am aware at once of the self and of the non-self, or that, as subject, I relate myself to, and distinguish myself from, the object. As Sartre states it: "every positional consciousness of an object is at the same time non-positional consciousness of itself."

This must be true of pre-reflective consciousness as well as of reflective consciousness.

What can this consciousness of consciousness be? We might be tempted at first to make of it another sort of positional consciousness, the idea of an idea, which could only be conceived through our having the idea of an idea of idea, and thus lead us into infinite regress. My being conscious of the existence of the table does not mean that I know I am conscious of that existence and that I am that knowledge. Consciousness is not to be confused with knowledge; knowledge is reflective consciousness but there is also a pre-reflective consciousness. In pre-reflective, or immediate consciousness, no doubt, I must be conscious at once of the object perceived and of myself as perceiving that object, but while I perceive the object, I do not take a position in regard to my consciousness of it. I may count the cigarettes left in my case without knowing that I am counting. My attention is turned outside, toward the cigarettes. If someone asks me: "What are you doing?" I answer: "I am counting my cigarettes," and I know myself counting. Pre-reflective consciousness is the condition which makes reflective consciousness possible. Reflective consciousness may react to pre-reflective consciousness and make me ashamed, proud, or afraid of what I have just perceived.

Descartes' "I think, therefore I am" should be applied to pre-reflective consciousness.

5

We should not think, therefore, that pre-reflective consciousness is primarily knowledge, a "thinking substance," like Descartes' *cogito*. In it we reach being and find an absolute, beyond which it is impossible to go. Since this absolute is an absolute of existence, not of knowledge, "it escapes that famous objection, according to which an absolute known is no longer an absolute because it becomes relative to the knowledge you take of it." [5] It appears to us as a total vacuum since the whole world is outside of it, yet "it is on account of that identity in it of appearance and existence that it may be considered as an absolute." [6] Descartes is right in saying: "I think, therefore I am," but everything capsizes when he defines his being as a "thinking substance." His mistake consists in not having distinguished between reflective and pre-reflective consciousness.

3. Being in itself.

The transphenomenality of the being of consciousness demands that of the being of the phenomenon.

Having found being in the pre-reflective consciousness of the observer (or *percipiens*), Sartre wonders whether the fact that the observer *is* could not in some way testify to the reality of the world of appearances which surrounds him. He rejects the idealistic view that a thing *is* merely because it is perceived (*esse est percipi*), for this would give it a passive existence, relative to consciousness. Even as an appearance, the object perceived stands outside of consciousness. To say that every consciousness is consciousness of something does not mean that it creates what it is conscious of, nor that its being is identical with the being of the thing perceived. "To be conscious *of*

6

something is to be facing a full and concrete presence which *is not* consciousness." [7]

The absence of most of the possible appearances within a given series constitutes the transphenomenal being of the phenomenon.

Now, of course, we can be conscious of an absence, but that absence appears necessarily on a background of presence: a person, for instance, can only be absent from actual surroundings where his presence could have been expected. Even in the perception of a present object, consciousness cannot fuse with the object of its intentionality because, as we have seen, no given series of appearances can ever be exhausted. Most of them must remain absent from the field of perception. Paradoxically, it is the absence of all the possible appearances of the object except one which gives the object its reality and constitutes the "transphenomenal being of the phenomenon." [8]

Consciousness questions its own being inasmuch as that being implies a being other than itself.

Consciousness has no being outside of its intentionality. To say that consciousness is consciousness of something is to say that it must reveal a being other than itself, already existing as it is revealed. We might apply to consciousness Heidegger's definition of the *Dasein*: "*Consciousness is a being for which there is a question of its being in its being,*" but we should add: "*inasmuch as that being implies a being other than itself.*" [9] This being is the transphenomenal being of the phenomenon. It is not a mysterious essence or noumenon hiding the phenomenon: it is the being of this or that object, of the

7

world generally, implied by our consciousness of them as we have seen. It is being-in-itself.

Sartre rejects both realism and idealism. Consciousness, as be-ing-for-itself, and its object, as being-in-itself, constitute a structure. Yet, these two modes of being are in some way irreducible. Being-in-itself, to Sartre, means being as such.

Sartre's quest of being thus leads him to reject both the idealist's and the realist's position: he discards realism by showing that the self-awareness of consciousness is distinct from awareness of the object and is implied by that awareness; he discards idealism by disclaiming that this self-awareness precedes and constitutes awareness of the object. His own position is therefore neither idealism nor realism. It is the position of common sense, insofar as it leads him to the common sense view concerning the ultimate reality of the outside world, as distinct from our awareness of it. We do not need to ground the reality of the world in a divine subjectivity, as Descartes does. Even if the world had been created, it would still have to fuse with that subjectivity or have its support in itself. We can, however, apply to being a reasoning somewhat similar to Descartes' proof of the existence of God through the idea of perfection. Just as Descartes uses the idea of a perfection *which is not in us* to prove that this idea must necessarily come from a being which has perfection, we can derive being from our awareness of being, since the reality of the world which surrounds us cannot be reduced to our awareness of it. What can be the relation between being and our awareness of it? This question remains to be answered and can only be answered through a further examination of the structure of consciousness. All we can do at this stage is

8

distinguish between being as such, being-in-itself, and this awareness of ourself as consciousness which we found to be distinct from our awareness of the object. How does being-in-itself appear to us if we distinguish it from the self-questioning being of consciousness?

Being is, being is in itself, being is what it is.

First of all, being-in-itself *is.* The principle of non-contradiction strictly applies to it. *It is what it is,* and the principle of identity also is valid here. It has no inside and no outside, it is massive. It has no becoming. It does not know of otherness. Having neither past nor future, it escapes temporality. Finally, it escapes both possibility and necessity: it simply *is* and will for that reason appear to consciousness as contingent. [not *logically* *necessary*] Being is, being is in itself, being is what it is, concludes Sartre, "these are the three characters which a preliminary examination of the phenomenon of being permits us to assign to the being of phenomena." [10] Thus having divested being-in-itself of all the characters which properly belong to consciousness, or being-for-itself, Sartre is now ready for a close examination of the latter. His manner of proceeding is not essentially different from that of Descartes doubting the reality of all things and discovering in this very doubt the reality of his existence, nor is it different from Husserl's "bracketing" of the world in order to study the operation of consciousness. His determination to remain on the plane of being has led him, however, to discover two distinct ways of being: being as such, or being-in-itself, and consciousness, or being-for-itself.

9

II   *Being-For-Itself*

1. Negation and non-being.

The relation between being-in-itself and being-for-itself may be defined as questioning; I question my presence in the world as consciousness.

Sartre's quest has led him so far to discover two irreducible aspects of being: being-in-itself and being-for-itself: roughly the reality of the world of consciousness outside and the absolute character of consciousness, another reality beyond which it is impossible to go; but he has not yet connected these two forms of being, although he has given us more than one hint concerning the rapport between them. What is the relationship between man-as-consciousness and the world which surrounds him? The answer must be sought within the question. If I am able to question the nature of my presence in the world, no doubt the relationship may already be defined as interrogation. What am I, for me to be able to question my existence?

10

Interrogation implies the possibility of a negation; negation involves the idea of non-being.

Any questioning process implies the possibility of a negative answer, were it only: "There is *no* answer to the question." It also implies the ignorance of the questioner; questioning is like a bridge thrown between two non-beings. Even if the answer is positive: "It is that way and *not* otherwise," it implies a non-being of limitation. Interrogation, then, implies the possibility of a negation; negation implies the existence, if one may say so, of a non-being.

Yet, non-being is not merely the product of negation.

Where does non-being come from? At first sight it could not come from being as such since this is full positivity. In other words, you could not find in the world something which is not there. Should we say that non-being is a pseudo-idea derived from negation and resting upon negative judgments? Shall we conclude that non-being is merely the negation of being, and therefore pure subjectivity?

"There is a transphenomenality of non-being, as of being." [11]

Sartre's answer could hardly be overstressed since it provides us with the key to his philosophy. The questioning attitude, whether manifested in words or not, expresses a rapport between being-in-itself and consciousness and is a purely human form of behavior. When I have engine trouble, "if I question the carburetor, it is because I consider it possible that *'there is nothing'* the matter with the carburetor. Thus my questioning involves by nature a certain prejudicative comprehension of non-being; it is in itself a relation of being with non-being, on the background of the original transcendence, i.e., of a relation of being with being." [12] We should not be misled by the fact that we mostly formulate our questioning, or negating, when talking to others. Destruction is a way of negating being, and only man destroys. Nature merely rearranges. Only man conceives of things as destructible, or as fragile, i.e., easily destroyed, turned into the non-being which is one of their possibilities. And yet, non-being is not a human invention. "It is indeed within the being of that vase that its fragility has been imprinted, and its destruction would be an irreversible and absolute event which I could merely observe." [13]

It is not true that negation can be reduced, as Bergson claims, to persistence of attention given an object which has been replaced by another; it is, rather, this persisting attention which contains a series of negations: 1) implicit negation of everything that is not its object, (Sartre borrows from Hegel and Spinoza the principle that every determination is a negation); 2) negation of the existence of that object in the image retained by consciousness (in his treatise on Imagination, Sartre explains that what distinguishes an image from a perception is the absence of its object); 3) negation of consciousness itself as being only that image. How can all these negations be related to the idea of non-being? Sartre takes as an illustration the feelings one experiences on not finding one's friend in the café where he has agreed to meet you. Upon arriving in the café, I look into the room, I see tables and people and I say: "He is not here." Has there been intuition of an absence or did the negation intervene only with my judgment? Certainly the café itself is a plenum of life, with its tables, mirrors, smoky atmosphere, the noises of people going and coming, the sound of conversations, the reflected lights, etc. But in perceiving, says Sartre, one isolates a form against a background. The café has become for me a background against which the image of my absent friend should stand out. I have questioned every face, looked into every corner, and thought: "That is not he," or: "He is not there." He is not absent from a definite spot, but from the whole café which has become half unreal, evanescent like the misty background with which some painters surround their portraits. In this case, the portrait itself is missing. The process by which I become aware of my friend's absence is a superposition of negations. I negate the café as I make it a background for my expectation; I negate the reality of the image evoked by that expectation; I negate my own consciousness which is that image.

Negation is somehow related to non-being.

Yet, I am responsible for this whole structure of negations. I caused them to surge between reality as it is given to me and myself:

> If anterior judgments are statements of fact . . . negation must be a sort of free invention; it must tear us away from this wall of positivity which hems us in: It is a sudden *break* in continuity which can in no case *result* from anterior affirmations, an original and irreducible event. But we are in the domain of consciousness. And consciousness can produce negation only under the form of consciousness of negation . . . The no, as a sudden intuitive discovery, appears as consciousness (of being), consciousness of the no. In a word, if there is being everywhere, it is not Non-being alone, as Bergson claims, which is inconceivable: from being, one will never derive negation. The necessary condi-

13

tion for it being possible to say *no* is that non-being be a perpetual presence in us and outside of us; it is that non-being should *haunt* being.[14]

Non-being haunts being, it emanates from our being, it is part of its very structure; the possibility of voiding, negating, nihilating is always with us. Our very perception of things consists in making a "form" stand against a "background," thereby attributing a sort of lesser existence to the background. It is a fact of daily experience that we freely confer non-being to facts, to things, to people, and even to fragments of our own experience, in the most arbitrary fashion. Belonging to "Society" consists, according to Proust, in ignoring the existence of that which is not "Society." Non-being, therefore, cannot be a pseudo-idea resulting from frustrated expectation, as Bergson would have us believe; nor could it be, as in Hegel, a pure abstraction which, joined with being also considered as a pure abstraction, would constitute becoming. Pure being is not a pure and transcendental abstraction for Sartre: it *is,* while non-being *is not.* Heidegger's conception of being and non-being as two antagonistic forces, producing a tension which is the basis of concrete realities, advances beyond Hegel. At least, Heidegger refrains from attributing to non-being the sort of reality which constitutes being. He does not say that non-being *is,* he merely states that "nothing nihilates." Nothingness, for him, is a sort of negating force, supported and conditioned by a movement of transcendence. This means that, in order to view his own contingency, his limitations, his finitude as a human being in the world, man has, so to speak, to leap into nothingness, into non-being. Daily experience testifies to our sense of nothingness, this nothingness which is the source of anguish. This conception, however, represents the world as being suspended within nothingness. Now, according to Sartre, if man can have the power to emerge into non-being, it is because he has first denied that he is the world and that he is himself. In this sense Hegel is right in affirming that Mind is the negative, but he does not explain how negativity operates as an essential structure of the human mind. To Sartre, as we have seen, non-being is implicit in every form of negation. It is also implicit in interrogation, since by interrogating we place the object of our query in a neutral state between being and non-being. It is implicit in determination, since, by limiting an object, we assign non-being to that object as its contour. Moreover, between absolute negativity and absolute positivity there is a whole gradation of intermediary states which Sartre calls "négatités." Let us note, in passing, that Sartre's study of these "négatités" throws an interesting light on human behavior. It is quite certain that some people affirm themselves mainly through negative behavior, that is, through direct, modified, or implicit negation.

2. Non-being and liberty.

Liberty comes from non-being because non-being escapes causality.

If non-being can be conceived neither *from* being nor *outside* of it, how does the notion of non-being originate? Sartre seeks the answer to this question in the questioning process itself:

Being could only engender being and, if man is completely involved (*englobé*) in this generating process, nothing but being will issue from him. For him to be able to ask himself a question about this process, i.e., to question it, he must be able to survey it as a totality, i.e., to place himself *outside*

15

of being and in so doing weaken the structure of being within being. Yet, it is not given to "human reality" to reduce to naught, even temporarily, the mass of being which confronts it. What it can modify is its *rapport* with that being. For "human reality," to place out of circuit a particular existant is to place itself out of circuit in relation to that existant. In this case, it escapes from the existant, gets out of reach, . . . withdraws *beyond a non-being*. Descartes, following the Stoics, gave a name to this possibility for human reality to secrete a non-being which isolates it: it is liberty.[15]

Liberty is not a property belonging to the essence of the human being: "There is no difference between the being of man and his 'being free.' "[16] To tear himself from the world and its causality, man must tear himself from himself first, and it is, so to speak, his very nature to do so. As soon as you disintegrate consciousness into a causal sequence, you reintegrate it within the "unlimited totality of being" as shown by "the vain efforts of psychological determinism to dissociate itself from universal determinism and to constitute a series apart."[17] Negation can neither come from perception, since we do not perceive non-being; nor from the missing being, unless we admit that this image involves a triple negation: negation of the world to which the object belongs as it vanishes into a background, negation of the presence of the object on that background, and implicit negation of any present reality corresponding to its image. Although he admits Husserl's intentional consciousness, Sartre does not accept his distinction between "full" and "empty" intentions. Both types of perceptions require, to become conscious, "a negative moment through which consciousness, in the absence of any anterior determination, constitutes itself into a negation":

16

In conceiving, from my conception of the room in which he lived, the one who is no longer in the room, I am quite necessarily brought to do an act of thought which no anterior state can determine nor motivate, to operate, in short, within myself, a rupture with being. And, inasmuch as I continually make use of *"négatités"* to isolate and determine the existants, i.e., to think them, the succession of my "consciousnesses" is a perpetual unhinging (*décrochage*) of the effect from the cause, since every negating process requires drawing its source from itself alone. . . . Any psychic process of negating implies therefore a split between the immediate psychic past and the present. This split is precisely non-being.[18]

It is useless to try finding determination within the negating process itself. The negating process escapes the cause-to-effect relationship, but cannot motivate a second negating: "A being can *negate* itself perpetually, but insofar as it negates itself, it renounces being the origin of another phenomenon, were it even a second negating." [19]

We now have to define further this sudden interruption, this separation between our "states of consciousness," which is the condition of negation. It is neither a break of continuity in the temporal flux, nor an opaque element which severs the anterior moment from the posterior, as the blade of a knife splits a fruit in two, nor is it a weakening of the motivating force of our consciousness. It strictly is *nothing*. The anterior consciousness is still there, modified by its past character, but it has been "bracketed," to use the expression of the phenomenologists. The nothingness which separates the present from the past is human consciousness, which is also consciousness of non-being:

It must be that the conscious being constitutes himself in relation to his past as separated from this past by a non-

17

being; it must be that he is consciousness of that split of being, but not as a phenomenon which he undergoes: rather as a structure of consciousness which he is.[20]

If consciousness is a kind of negating force, it must be consciousness of negation and of non-being. "We should be able to define and describe a perpetual mode of consciousness, present *as* consciousness, which would be consciousness of negating." And if liberty is the being of consciousness, consciousness must involve a consciousness of liberty. There must be "a certain way to stand before one's past and one's future as being, at once, that past and that future, and of not being them." [21] There is indeed and it is *anguish*.

3. Liberty and anguish.

Anguish is awareness of our liberty and of the non-being which makes it possible.

Kierkegaard derives anguish from liberty, Heidegger from consciousness of non-being. There is no contradiction between these definitions: they imply each other. Fear is my apprehension of the beings in this world; anguish is my apprehension of self. Dizziness before a precipice is anguish insofar as I fear, not to fall over the precipice, but to throw myself over it. Dizziness is an example of anguish before the future. It may start with fear: fear of an unpredictable incident which will make me fall. Fear will make me envisage various possibilities of behavior which will reduce the possibilities of my fall. But these possibilities of behavior are not determined by any anterior conduct, otherwise they would cease being possibilities. So long as they remain mere possibilities the other possibility also remains: that of letting myself fall over the

18

precipice. No doubt, I tend toward my own safety, away from it, in the near future; but I am separated from that near future by a non-being. I feel that nothing can prevent me from jumping over the precipice. Fortunately, the possibility of doing so is going to suggest to me determining reasons why I should do so and the very fact that these reasons appear as motives will permit me to reject them as ineffective.

There is another sort of anguish which is anguish before the past. It is that of the gambler who has decided never to gamble any more, and who realizes, as he approaches the gambling table, that he is as desperately free to do so as ever. The resolution not to play is still there, but it is inefficient because the gambler is aware of it as being:

"sicklied o'er with the pale cast of thought."

He has to refuse himself the possibility of playing again through a new decision, "ex nihilo."

Consciousness stands before the Ego's past and future as being neither, and yet as having to assume them.

Consciousness then "is not its own motive since it is empty of all contents. This sends us back to a nihilating structure of the pre-reflective *cogita";* furthermore, "consciousness is before its past and its future as before a self which it is on the mode of not being it. This sends us back to a nihilating structure of temporality." [22] The liberty which anguish reveals to us "is characterized by a perpetually renewed obligation to make over again the Ego which designates the free being." [23] The Ego, with its given and historical contents, must be recreated with each situation. It is the essence of man; but

19

man is always separated from his essence by a non-being. "Essence is what has been. . . . But the act is always beyond that essence . . . because everything which can be designated in man by the formula: this is, by that very fact *has been*.[24] Hegel is right in saying: *"Wesen ist was gewesen ist."*

We flee anguish through the spirit of seriousness, psychological determinism, belief in a deeper Ego which produces our action as father begets son, or bad faith, which consists in making ourself conscious of anguish to get rid of it.

How is it that anguish is so seldom felt in all its acuity? Because we often learn our possibilities as we make them realities. They are subordinated to a wider project to which we have committed ourselves, and which we prefer not to question. Moreover, we accept social values and taboos as we accept life itself. As soon as circumstances cause us to be left entirely to ourselves, we realize that we make values and we cease finding moral support in the "spirit of seriousness," which consists in seeking reasons in the nature of things for action, in believing that values are somehow attached to them, as a "How to Use" leaflet instructs us in the use of a newly bought piece of merchandise. Anguish is the sense we have of our freedom to accept or reject values. Our main line of conduct toward anguish is flight. The spirit of seriousness, by which we ask the things of this world to dictate us our behavior, is only the most elementary and spontaneous form of flight from anguish. Psychological determinism is a somewhat more sophisticated form of escape on the reflective plane. It recognizes within us the presence of antagonistic forces comparable to physical forces. It does away with the feeling of consciousness as non-being. We just witness the interplay within us

20

of various forces comparable to those which move things around us, and find it reassuring to share the existence of things, without inquiring what privileged gallery has been assigned our consciousness for the enjoyment of the spectacle. The Bergsonian sense of liberty is an even more refined form of escape. It consists in conceiving of liberty as a continuous and harmonious development of the Ego. The deeper and subconscious self, as it organizes itself through homogeneous duration, produces our actions as a father engenders his progeny. They become the natural manifestation of our historically constituted selves, of all that we have been in the past, without any break in the continuity of our psychic life. This kind of liberty, Sartre asserts, is not the liberty we feel within us, it is the liberty we grant others. It is conceived not on the existential, but on the biological plane. It is "a projection of the liberty—which we feel in us—into a psychic object which is the Ego." [25] The two objections, then, which Sartre presents to the Bergsonian conception of liberty are that, in it, the free act is a natural outcome of psychic duration, therefore springing from the past, and that it eliminates the break in continuity, the negative moment through which we have to pass in our transcendence toward the future. Finally, there is another means of escape which consists in becoming conscious of our anguish, so that the nihilating character of consciousness may permit us to take a more detached attitude toward it, to view it, as it were, from outside, as one gets rid of one's inhibitions. But, of course, "I must think of it constantly in order to take care not to think of it" [26] as I take to flight toward the "reassuring myths." This is what Sartre calls "bad faith." In bad faith we *are* anguish in order to flee anguish. In this peculiar behavior, we seem to find within a single consciousness the unity of being and non-being. The

21

study of bad faith gives precious indications about the problem of non-being and the part it plays in human consciousness.

4. From anguish to bad faith: to be in order not to be.

By making ourselves conscious of our states of mind, we objectify them and dissociate ourselves from them.

We have seen already that in our first movement of transcendence toward the object, we at once affirm the existence of the thing aimed at and deny that we are that thing: consciousness appears to itself as not being its object. We found "non-being as the condition of transcendence toward being." [27] In bad faith, on the contrary, we find that we are anguish in order not to be anguish, as if we had a pre-reflective intuition that on the plane of consciousness we are not what we are. What can consciousness be to allow the existence of bad faith?

In so doing, we are lying to ourselves. We establish a duality where there is none. The theory of the subconscious stresses that duality, but experience shows that the censor and the censored are one.

We should first of all distinguish bad faith from lying. Lying implies the existence of others. Bad faith is lying to oneself. The liar and the person lied to are the same person. Various explanations, one being the theory of the subconscious, have been offered to establish the duality of deceiver and deceived. In psychoanalysis, the subconscious is censored by consciousness; but the censor, in spite of its willingness to consider objectively the facts submitted to it, often shows a resistance to accept them which proves that the censor and the censored are one. The inhibited tendency could not disguise itself under a symbolic form if it did not involve: 1) the consciousness of being inhibited, 2) the consciousness of having been rejected because it is what it is, 3) a project of disguise." [28] To Sartre, the gratification of suppressed desires through symbols involves "an obscure comprehension of the aim to be reached, inasmuch as it is simultaneously desired and forbidden." [29] The subconscious does not explain bad faith.

Confession of guilt is another attempt to find duality in ourselves.

The man who says: "I hate myself for acting the way I do," and considers this admission as a sort of justification, is asking you to consider only his transcendent self, the self he hopes to be some day, the self he is not; he is trying to convince himself that he is not his present self: *I*, the subject, a pure and innocent consciousness, deny that I am *myself*, the object of my contempt, through that very objectivation. I am not what I am, and am what I am not, and I depend on you, as a fellow human being, to grasp this mystery without effort. To the extent to which I deceive myself in this process, I am in bad faith. I disavow my actual behavior and ask to be considered as a mere spectator of that behavior; but where is that invisible gallery from which I have the privilege of beholding my misbehavior?

Playing at being what we really are is another attempt to find duality in ourselves.

To take another example, very entertainingly presented by Sartre himself, let us consider the way in which this café waiter plies his trade, the neat and precise automatism of all his gestures, the ease of his obsequious politeness, the way in which he links an action to the next as if in emulation of a smooth-running piece of machinery, the slight stylization he seems to impart to his every action. He seems to be playing a part and to be amused by that part as if it were a game. What sort of a game is he playing? Obviously, he is playing at being a café waiter, which is what he is, and what others want him to be. He plays the waiter as the actor plays Hamlet; he represents a waiter, to others and to himself. By the mere fact that he is trying to play a part, he places himself beyond that part, he confers on it a sort of unreality, a sort of non-being. Should we conclude, as does one critic, that it is not the waiter but Sartre himself who is entertaining himself at our expense? Not if we consider the peculiar delight human nature experiences in standing on the borderline between being and non-being, between reality and make-believe. Anyone may find an infinite number of examples bearing on this fact within his own experience; and the spectacle of long lines of human beings waiting for the privilege of devouring shadows in a cinema as a fitting reward for the week's labor, is a gross but striking image of our capacity for self-delusion.

To realize absolute sincerity toward oneself seems an impossible task to Sartre. To be sincere is to be what one is; which presupposes that one generally is not what one is, but should and could be. But the very structure of consciousness makes it impossible for us to form a definite idea of ourselves from past experience and to conform to that idea since, by becoming conscious of what we are, we transcend that knowledge, not towards another way of being but towards nothingness. Anyone can experience the intuition of this fact through the uneasiness one experiences in trying to be "true to oneself." By recognizing "the facts about ourselves," (what Sartre would call our "facticity"), we refuse to be defined by such facts. This is why "a sin confessed is half forgiven." By cutting himself from his past behavior, through a kind of objectification of himself, the sinner ceases to be what he confesses to be. We consider the negative character Sartre attributes to consciousness as a sort of paradox; yet its neutralizing force is so well recognized by all forms of mental or spiritual disciplines, extending from Freudianism to Christian Science, that this point should not need stressing. Sincerity, inasmuch as it tries to make me appear at once as what I am and as what I am not, pursues the same aims as bad faith. Both imply that "human reality," even before it becomes reflective, is what it is not, and is not what it is.

5. Consciousness is not what it is; it is presence to self.

Even as immediate awareness, consciousness involves self-awareness, but denies being that immediate awareness. It is a reflecting reflection.

How can consciousness at once be and not be? Why does it seem to be running away from itself? "It has often been said that the reflective look alters the fact of consciousness on which it is directed." [30] Sartre accepts neither Spinoza's recourse to the infinite regress of the idea of an idea, nor Hegel's introduction of infinity within consciousness; he seeks reflectivity within immediate awareness. From its origin, consciousness escapes from itself. Consciousness is reflection, but as a reflection it is also reflecting. How can we explain this strange

25

duality of being for itself? First of all, what is the "self"? The self marks an ideal distance within the immanence of the subject, in relation to itself, a way of not being itself, of escaping identity while positing it as unity, of not coinciding with itself, "of being in a perpetually unstable equilibrium between identity as absolute cohesion . . . and unity as the synthesis of a multiplicity." [31] Again, we may think of the man who says: "I hate myself for acting that way," as illustrating this definition of the self, although his case may involve a form of social consciousness with which we are not yet familiar. Generally, it discloses the way reflective consciousness has of standing before itself as not being itself.

It is merely present to itself. The principles of identity and of non-contradiction do not apply to it.

This is what Sartre calls the "presence to the self" of consciousness. To be present to something implies that you are not that something. Consciousness exists as presence to itself at an ideal distance from itself, as not being itself, as its own negation. The principle of identity does not apply to consciousness. "It can only denote the rapports of being with *the exterior,* since precisely it rules the rapports of being with what it (being) is not." The principle of non-contradiction deals with *"external relations,* such as they may appear to a human reality present to being-in-itself and engaged in the world; it does not concern the internal rapports of being. . . . The principle of identity is the negation of any sort of relation within being-in-itself. On the contrary, presence to self implies that an imperceptible fissure has crept into being. If it is present to itself, it is not quite itself. Presence is an immediate degradation of coincidence, for it presupposes separation." [32]

26

What separates consciousness from being is strictly nothing, *or rather it is a self-nihilation.*

What separates being from being may be time or space or some sort of qualified difference. In this case, if we wonder what separates the subject from itself, we have to admit that it is *nothing*. Between a belief and the consciousness of a belief, there is nothing else but that consciousness. If you try to grasp the separation, it vanishes, and you are referred to pure belief; if you try to grasp the belief as such, the fissure is there again. That fissure is a pure negative. It is nothing, yet it can nihilate. It is non-being. But again, you can hardly say that non-being "is." If the verb "to be" could be used passively, you should rather say that it "is been" (*qu'il est été.*) In other words, the non-being of consciousness is borne by being. The belief which degrades itself into consciousness of belief denies that it is that belief.

6. Consciousness is what it is not: that is its facticity.

Consciousness has its facticity and it is the contingency of the being in itself.

Yet consciousness is. It is as an event, it is:

". . . in the same sense as I may say that Philip II *has been,* that my friend Pierre is; it is inasmuch as it appears in a condition which it has not chosen, inasmuch as Pierre is a French bourgeois of 1942, as Schmidt *was* a Berliner and a workman of 1870; it *is* inasmuch as it is thrown into a world, abandoned in a situation; it is inasmuch as it *is* pure contingency, inasmuch as for him, as for the things of the world, as for that wall, that tree, that cup, the original question may arise: 'Why is this being such and not otherwise?' It *is*, inasmuch as there is in it something the foundation of which it is not: its *presence to the world*." [33]

Consciousness has to assume the contingency of being-in-itself, since it has no foundation of its own.

This discovery of one's contingency is in any *cogito*. Descartes implies it in the realization of his imperfection: "I think, therefore I am." What am I? I am a being which is not its own foundation since it has the idea of perfection, perfection which is nowhere to be found. But this does not mean that its contingency is grounded in another being who is necessary and perfect. It means that being-in-itself, which is contingent, can only become its own foundation by becoming for-itself. "The for-itself is the in-itself losing itself as in-itself in order to found itself as consciousness." [34] Since, however, the for-itself has no other reality, no other being than that of the in-itself which it reflects, it has to assume the contingency of the in-itself. It can only exist on the foundation of a given situation. To this situation, the for-itself (my consciousness), can give a sense; it cannot create this situation, being merely present to it. The situation is out of reach; yet, since consciousness, to be at all, has to assume it, consciousness is responsible for it. It represents what Sartre calls its "facticity." Although the café waiter may play at being a café waiter, he is still a café waiter. If he were playing at being a diplomat, that would not make him a diplomat.

The in-itself becomes the for-itself so as to become its own foundation, but retains its contingency.

Thus, "the for-itself is conscious of its facticity, it has the sentiment of its entire gratuitousness, it apprehends itself as

28

being there for nothing, as being in excess (*de trop*)." [35] In short, "Being-in-itself may ground its non-being, but not its being; in its decompression, it nihilates itself into a for-itself which becomes, as for-itself, its own foundation; but its contingency of being-in-itself remains out of reach." [36]

7. Being-in-itself-for-itself as the ideal value.

Being-for-itself is a lack of being. If the for-itself could acquire the concreteness of the in-itself, it would realize the ideal value of being at once in itself and for itself.

Being-for-itself could not at once negate and assume its contingency if it did not constitute itself as lack of being. The for-itself is a lack; the lack of that which would make it a complete self. Sartre's reasoning on this point somewhat resembles both that of Descartes arguing that man, who only knows of imperfect beings, yet tends toward a perfect being, or that of Pascal who derives the existence of an element of infinity within man from man's dissatisfaction with his relativity. For Sartre, the lack felt by consciousness is the lack of being; consciousness aims at a complete manner of being which would be at once in and for itself.

It would retain its lucidity and give to being a free foundation. This is impossible, yet such an ideal haunts human consciousness in the guise of the concept of God.

Consciousness, indeed, does not want to return to the identity of the pure but contingent in-itself, since then it would cease to be as consciousness. It tends toward coinciding with the in-itself without losing its lucidity. Its aim is to cease being a pure negation, a nothing, and to acquire the substance of the in-itself without ceasing to be for itself. Being-in-itself would then receive a free instead of a contingent foundation, and the being-in-itself-for-itself would realize the totality of the self. This totality is impossible through the very nature of being-in-itself and of being-for-itself. It is hypostatized in meditation under the concept of God. It haunts consciousness and is the origin of the unhappiness of consciousness.

We should not think, however, that this ideal value haunts consciousness merely as a pure abstraction. Concrete consciousness always emerges with a situation. A feeling, a pleasure, a pain, are, according to Sartre, felt as lack of being. We like the expression of suffering on a bronze mask because, to us, it is suffering solidified and concrete. When we manifest some sort of suffering, it is because we can only act that suffering, attempting to transform ourselves for others into statues of pain. Thus the disorderly gestures of a man in pain would not point to a desperate flight away from pain, but to a feeling of inadequacy on the part of consciousness to espouse the real pain which is its object. The ideal value toward which it tends is pain in itself and for itself.

Our sense of value constitutes an obligation to assume our contingency, but merely as a ground for consciousness and liberty.

Value, therefore, does not point to something transcendental, but merely to the absolute self, in and for itself; it is a sense of being, a thirst for being, but for being grounded in consciousness and in liberty. Consciousness *has to* assume the contingency of being in itself, but only as the foundation of its being in itself.

30

8. From value to possibilities.

There are possibilities only for consciousness.

"Being for itself cannot appear without being haunted by values and projected towards its particular possibilities." [37] What does Sartre mean by "possibilities"? "The surging of being-for-itself as negation of being-in-itself and as decompression of being, causes the possible to surge as one of the aspects of that decompression of being, i.e., as a manner of being what one is at a distance from oneself." [38] We sometimes project the idea of possibility into things. For instance, we say, after looking at the clouds: "It may rain," in which case we merely state our ignorance concerning certain data. There are possibilities only for a being, man, "who is to himself his own possibilities." [39] Only consciousness has possibilities, and it is these possibilities which disjoin it from its contingency. Even as I am reading this book, I am conscious not of reading letters, words, and paragraphs, but of reading the whole book. To reach the end of the book is my possibility, as it is to drop it if I come to feel that I am "getting nowhere" in reading it. My consciousness of reading the book does not merely refer to the pages already read, but also to the pages which I still must read.

Consciousness considers as its possibility its presence to an event it anticipates.

Consciousness, therefore, does not merely function as a sort of instantaneous witness. As presence to self, it anticipates its presence to a self which is not yet in being. As I become conscious that I am getting thirsty, I feel my thirst as a lack:

31

a lack of the drink which would quench my thirst. In satisfied thirst, the consciousness of thirst tends to realize its completion. The man who thirsts, according to Sartre, does not want the cessation of thirst, except on a purely reflective plane, i.e., on second thought; he wants to become conscious of satiated thirst. No consciousness wants its suppression. Love, even if it is unhappy, does not aim at the end of love. "What desire wants is a void filled, informing its repletion as the mold informs the bronze which has been cast in it." [40]

Consciousness does not tend merely toward coincidence with a particular this or that, but with the whole of being.

The coincidence of consciousness with being can, of course, never be complete. Consciousness is condemned to remain a mere presence to being, since it is negation of being. Moreover, consciousness does not aim merely at a particular being, but at the totality of being, the world, which it negates. In this sense, consciousness, as an absolute of negation, is separated from its full possibility by the whole world, and projects its coincidence with the whole world. This is what Sartre calls the "circuit of ipseity."

Consciousness transcends itself toward its possibilities without ceasing being itself, as an "ipseity," which unifies the world as the sum total of its possibilities. The sense of this movement is found in temporality.

Ipseity, or selfness, is not the Ego: the Ego is my self objectified. It is not consciousness, it appears as having been there before consciousness. This is not the case of the "I." Again, the case of the man who says: "I hate myself" might

32

roughly illustrate this point. The first movement of consciousness as presence to itself brings along a second movement, ipseity, which involves consciousness of my possibilities. It is not a mere reflection of the being-in-itself, nor of the being-for-itself. It refers to the presence of the self beyond all its possibilities; a presence which is also an absence. "What I seek as I face the world is coincidence with a being for itself which I am and which is consciousness *of the world*."[41] The world is filled with possibilities which are my possibilities, and it is these possibilities which give it its unity and its meaning as world. It is, however, in time that my possibilities appear at the horizon of the world which they make mine. It is in temporality that I must seek the sense of my transcendence toward my possibilities, as my consciousness, which rejects instantaneity, invites me to do.

9. Temporality.

Past, present, and future are parts of a single structure.

Temporality is obviously an organized structure, and these three so-called elements of time: past, present, future, must not be envisaged as a collection of 'data' to be added together —for instance, as an infinite series of 'nows' some of which are not yet, some of which are no more—but as the structured moments of an original synthesis. Otherwise we shall immediately meet with this paradox: the past is no longer, the future is not yet, as for the instantaneous present, everyone knows that it is not at all: it is the limit of infinite division, like the dimensionless point.[42]

The past is the in-itself which consciousness is not *but has to assume.*

33

THE PAST is not a mere nothing, but it exists only as a function of the present, bound with it and with a certain future. Any past is the past of something or of somebody. If I am talking of the past of someone who is dead, quite obviously such a past is past in relation to my own present. The relation of the present to the past is the relation of the for-itself to the in-itself, of consciousness to being. The past is the being which I am, inasmuch as I have passed beyond. It is facticity. It is that which I cannot change, although I can give it a new meaning through my actions until the moment of my death, at which time I shall be no more than a past, i.e., a pure in-itself for the consciousness of others. Such is the meaning of the line in which Mallarmé sees Poe:

"Such as into himself eternity changes him."

The present is the presence *of the for-itself to the in-itself which it denies being. It is the flight of consciousness from being.*

If the past is in itself, THE PRESENT is for itself. It refers to the *presence* of the for-itself to the in-itself, of consciousness to being, the whole of being, i.e., the world. Presence to a being implies that you are connected with that being by an internal subjective bond which is not identity. The present, then, is an ideal term; the present *is* not; it merely "presentifies" itself in the same way as Heidegger says that "nothing nihilates." As has often been said, the moment I try to grasp it, it sinks into the past. What really *is* is that being to which I am present: the dial of the clock when I am looking at the time, for example. The present of consciousness is a perpetual flight before being.

34

Consciousness, in that flight, projects itself as present, without loss of identity, toward a being which does not yet exist.

THE FUTURE is the meaning of that flight. There can be no future except for the being which is its own future,

the being which makes itself exist as having its being outside of itself, in the future. Let us take a simple example: this position which I quickly assume on the tennis court has no meaning except through the movement which I shall make afterwards with my racket to return the ball over the net. . . . It is the future gesture which . . . turns back on the positions which I adopt, to bring light upon them, link them and modify them.[43]

Finality is then, literally, causality in reverse. My gestures receive their meaning from the future. The for-itself makes itself present to the in-itself as lack of something—a possibility—which will make it a complete self. The for-itself and its lack are given within the unity of a single surge which is the consciousness of its future. There is no future outside of that consciousness through which the for-itself constitutes itself as not being what it is.

As it projects itself toward its possibilities (the future), consciousness wants to remain consciousness, i.e., a mere presence, and the same consciousness, identified by its past and by the whole moving world which is its background.

Let us remember, however, that consciousness does not wish to cease being for itself as it projects itself toward the realization of the complete self. It wants to remain a *presence* to being, and the same presence. The consciousness which projects wants to be present to the accomplishment of the project. "I shall be happy" means: "My present being-for-itself will be happy," with all the past that it drags behind. Thus what is generally revealed to consciousness is not a future way of being for itself, but a future world, and my project has to take place on the background of a world of motion. I may even attribute to this moving world the possibilities which I feel within myself, and this is the basis of determinism.

Consciousness aims at being simultaneously for itself and in itself.

But the future is something else besides the presence of the being-for-itself to a being situated beyond being. It is my self, as we have seen. "The future is the ideal point where the sudden and infinite compression of facticity (the past), of the for-itself (the present) and of its possible (to come) would at last cause the Self to surge as existence in itself of the for-itself." [44] To apprehend that such a realization is indeed the aim of consciousness, we need only try to imagine ourselves occupying at some future date the position of someone we envy; unless we can retain the identity which our past confers on us, our imagination will reject the idea, not merely because it seems absurd but also because it evokes spiritual death.

The realization of this project is impossible. Any particular project, once achieved, becomes a being-in-itself and slips back into the past.

Yet, the for-itself cannot be at the same time in itself. When a particular project which we have been aiming at in the future becomes a realized project, it slips back into the past as a pure in-itself, and constitutes a foundation from which the for-itself, realizing its nothingness, springs toward a new project and a new future. The complete self is unattainable.

Yet consciousness is condemned to be free and to choose among all possibilities those which it will make its possibilities.

The future is the sense of the for-itself. It *is* not, but merely makes itself possible without end. It remains problematical, since between consciousness and its possibilities there is the liberty consciousness derives from its non-being. As a conscious being, I am condemned to be free. Among all possibilities, I choose those which are *my* possibilities, even if, in order to come closer to them, I have to adopt, for purely rational reasons, some other possibilities which are merely means to an end. To pay a visit to a friend is my possibility, but whether I go by taxi or subway will depend merely on circumstances.

Temporality represents the dispersion of consciousness within a unifying act.

Therefore, the three dimensions of temporality: past, present and future, belong to the structure of consciousness. Their study constitutes the phenomenology of temporality. If we now try to ascertain what relations these dimensions, which are imposed by consciousness upon being, have with being, to define them in terms of being and non-being, we discover that they represent at once a dispersion and a unifying act of

37

consciousness. Each dimension corresponds to a kind of projection toward the mirage of the self. In its first dimension, consciousness negates itself, insofar as it *is* facticity, or factuality, and that facticity is left behind, objectified into a *past* being-in-itself. Being-in-itself is what being-for-itself (consciousness) was before. We now understand why the moments of temporality should appear to us as irreversible and distinct: as negation of the in-itself (being), the for-itself (non-being) must necessarily follow. It affirms itself through this separation somewhat in the same manner as it becomes aware of itself through negating that it is the object: my consciousness of the chair is aware of itself as consciousness through negation of the possibility that it is the chair. Yet there is a difference, because, in this case, the negation is internal, and because I have to assume my past at the same time that I make it my past, since my consciousness of self is borne by my past. In its second dimension, consciousness apprehends itself as a certain lack. The present never refers to a completed action: I drink is equivalent to I am drinking. So long as I am conscious of accomplishing a certain act, I cannot identify myself with that act with the full density of being; my consciousness is merely *present* to the accomplishment of the act. In its third dimension, consciousness escapes from that very presence by making itself present to a nonexistent accomplishment, or rather disperses itself in all directions, within the unity of a single flight. Temporality, therefore, is simply a way of being particular to consciousness.

The for-itself is the permanent element throughout change.

Definition of temporality as a single structure does not, however, eliminate the question of duration and becoming.

Why does a new being-for-itself take its place as the present of that past? What about the old Heraclitean problem of change? What about the dynamics of temporality? Change implies the permanence of that which changes, say Leibniz and Kant. Certainly, says Sartre, but that permanence is conferred from outside by a witness and is therefore in the witness. Duration is in the being-for-itself. If we consider what happens when the present becomes a past, we notice that it immediately brings into existence a new present which becomes the present of that past (a past is always related to a present). The past of that past at once becomes its pluperfect; but past and pluperfect are really bound together within the being-in-itself. Meanwhile, the future of the new present either remains ahead if it is a distant future, or becomes the present, in which case it remains future in relation to the past while becoming present. The reflection: "So, this is what I was waiting for," expresses the feeling which attends the realization of that change. If the future remains distant, it still retains the character of given possibility, but it is an objectified possibility which is no longer my possibility; it is a possibility related to a lack felt by a past being, which is now in itself. That future appears to me with the character of a being-in-itself. It still has a character of ideality, but that ideality is in itself. It would be a mistake to consider the metamorphosis of present into past as the replacement of a being-in-itself by another; the new present negates the former present inasmuch as it has become in-itself. Being-for-itself, then, is constantly absorbed by being. Its non-being is expelled, or rather remains only as a quality of the being-in-itself. A past sadness is no longer an appearance which consciousness may reflect at will; it is an event to be accepted objectively as belonging to a past world, lost in universal de-

39

terminism. The present is like a vacuum of being constantly refilled by being, a perpetual flight before the being-in-itself which threatens to swamp, or suck in, the being-for-itself, until death consecrates the ultimate triumph of being-in-itself.

The permanence of being-for-itself which can only be explained by its spontaneity, which is one of refusal, explains the irreversibility of temporality: the order "positing-refusing" cannot be reversed.

The conception of an organized temporality constitutes a definite progress over that of the "instant" framed between a past which is no more and a future which is not yet. The instant now moves escorted by its present and its future; yet, this very movement has not been explained. The "instant" has simply been replaced by the totality of the structure: past, present, future. And since Sartre has defined the present as the mere presence of the being-for-itself, i.e., as non-being, time still may be considered as a dream. The passage from one instant to the next—since the instant is still the unreal pivot of the whole structure—remains to be explained. It can only be explained through the spontaneity of the being-for-itself; a spontaneity which is at once the foundation of its non-being and of its being:

And it is precisely its spontaneous character which constitutes the very irreversibility of its escapes since, as soon as it appears, it is a self-refusal, and since the order "positing-refusing" cannot be reversed.[45]

Once objectified, a past being-for-itself remains for consciousness, but merely as a contingency.

The spontaneity of the being-for-itself explains why it should endure as the permanent witness of that which is:

> The flight of the for-itself is a refusal of contingency through the very act which constitutes it as being the foundation of its non-being. But it is precisely that flight which constitutes as contingency that which is fled: the for-itself which has been fled (*le pour-soi fui*) is left on the spot. It could not disappear completely (*s'anéantir*) since I *am* it, neither can it but be the foundation of its own non-being since it can be that only in flight: it is *accomplished*.[46]

And so, the time of consciousness is a human reality which makes itself temporal as unachieved totality; and the whole of temporality is a negation of the instant.

10. Reflection.

Reflection is consciousness trying to become aware of itself. The relation between reflective consciousness and reflected consciousness is the same as that between being-for-itself and being-in-itself, but it is quite unstable and leads to being for others.

Outside of the dimensions of time, I feel in myself the unity I confer on a succession of events; I feel myself lasting; I feel the flow of time. What connection is there between time as a structure, the original temporality, and psychic duration? Obviously, when we think of duration as a succession of events we are no longer dealing with immediate consciousness, but with reflection. Reflection is the being-for-itself conscious of itself, the consciousness of consciousness. Yet, it is not a new consciousness born out of nothing, the old *idea of an idea* of Spinoza; *reflective* consciousness is one with *re-*

41

flected consciousness. Otherwise we could not understand its intuitive privileges. The reflective must *be* the reflected, but the relation between them must be a subject to object relation of the same kind as the relation between being-in-itself and being-for-itself, which means the separation implied by knowledge. By this very separation, the being-for-itself should become object for the reflective being. But the being-for-itself is already a reflection; reflection of the being-for-itself upon itself, which makes it for-itself-for-itself (being the reflection of a reflection, the shadow of a shadow), is an unstable mode of being leading directly to *being-for-others.*

Pure reflection preserves the dimensions of time; impure reflection forgets them in its attempt to objectify past consciousness.

Reflection, in its relation with temporality, may be pure or impure. To pure reflection, the three dimensions of time should appear as they have been described above. The being-for-itself is revealed to it as the quest of an unattainable self, on the mode of a particular selfness, or ipseity, i.e., as a private history, as historicity. In its impure form, reflection is "the concrete weaving of psychic units of duration":[47] a joy appears after a sadness coming after a humiliation. Of these we make psychic objects stretched out along the canvas of our time with mere exterior relations. Or else we admit their relativity: a stroke of thunder heard after a long silence has a peculiar quality which makes of it the "stroke-of-thunder-heard-after-a-long-silence," but we do not thereby explain it. Alone the being-for-itself can explain it: alone the being-for-itself can yearn for itself in the future, dragging its past along.

Impure reflection conceives the being-for-itself as the psyche.

Reflection appears to us primarily in its impure form, and we have to work a catharsis to find it in its pure form. Impure reflection tends to be the being-for-itself as in itself. It tries to grasp the reflected as in itself, yet claims identity with it, and is, to that extent, bad faith. Thus can we say: "Love, anger, made me act in such a way," as if love or anger were entities exterior to our subjectivity. In that case, reflection is first of all an effort to see ourselves as others see us, and leads to "being for others." What reflection perceives then is not an authentic process of temporalization but the "psyche."

The psyche comprises the qualities, states, and acts of the person. These constitute the objects of psychological research.

By psyche, Sartre means the Ego, its qualities, states, and acts. The Ego, under the grammatical forms *I* and *me,* represents our person as distinct from other persons, but still related to them. Its qualities: ambition, courage, etc., are latent ways of being. Its habits are qualities derived from personal history: we may have acquired tastes, distastes, etc., through circumstances. A state of being may become a quality: from having become angry, I may retain a latent disposition to get angry. The acts comprise the disposition of means toward an end. These qualities, states, and acts are perceived as objects by psychological research. Indeed, they may be called objects since they stand before our reflective consciousness as such; I may reflect on a past love and describe it, knowing all along that I no longer feel that love.

The conception of the psyche as a succession or as an inter-penetration of states of mind within the unity of the Ego involves a contradiction. In neither case is their interaction explained. Psychic causality is a spurious concept resulting from the projection of the being-for-itself into the being-in-itself. Psychology should limit itself to the description of psychic irrationality.

The psyche retains the three dimensions of past, present, and future, but as a succession of "nows," given as successive data within a single psyche. Hence a contradiction, since the "nows" are considered as entities within the unity of a single organism. The fact is that this unity is only that of the being-for-itself hypostatized in the being-in-itself. Bergson's "interpenetration of states of consciousness" refers to the psyche, not to the being-for-itself. Bergsonian duration is passively and unknowingly lived until intuition reveals it. The reproach of considering states of consciousness as inert data, so often made by Bergson to traditional psychology, is turned by Sartre against Bergson himself. Not that Sartre denies entirely the possibility of an interpenetration of "states of consciousness"; a friendship may have elements of love in it, but as long as it does not make itself love it remains as an inert object for which language has no name. The psychic process implies the action of anterior states of mind on posterior states of mind, an action which remains unexplained, either by interpenetration or by motivation. If there is penetration, we have a synthesis of two states of mind, both of which remain unaltered; if there is motivation, we have a kind of magical action exercised at a distance by one state on another. Thus, in Proust, the disappearance of jealousy makes room for the craving of certain sensations which creates the need of a certain presence. Various feelings, considered as objectified forces, act on each other like chemical agents, but in a completely irrational way.

44

There is no reason why one state of mind should bring about the next unless we want to have it that way. The psychologist should not try to establish the mechanics of psychic causality; he should be satisfied to describe psychic irrationality. Psychic causality is a spurious conception resulting from the projection of the being-for-itself, and of original temporality, into the being-in-itself. Psychic causality disappears if the in-itself remains on the non-reflective plane, or if reflection purifies itself. How it can purify itself, Sartre does not yet tell us.

The psyche is only in the same manner as a given situation is; the liberty of the being-for-itself is always beyond, although liberty can manifest itself only from a given situation. "Internal" duration is an illusion.

For the time being, let us note that he does not deny the reality of the psyche; my psyche *is*, since it reveals itself to my consciousness. It is like my shadow: what I see of myself when I want to *see* myself. But it *is* only as a *situation*, even if that situation is quite real for the being-for-itself, which, in fact, can take its free leap into a transcendent future only from a given situation. Let us remember also that reflection confers on the data of the psyche a kind of duration which is the original temporality degraded into a sort of being-in-itself: a sense of "internal" or "qualitative" duration. The being-for-itself, through reflection, may seem to have reached a fairly concrete form, which is like a first sketch of the portrait it will seek in the consciousness of others. But this is only an illusion. The being-for-itself exists primarily as transcendence.

45

III   Being-In-The-World

1. Knowledge.

*Every knowledge is intuitive; it is the presence of conscious-
ness to the thing. This implies that consciousness is not what
it is present to, and that knowledge is merely a negative mode
of being.*

Before treating, under the heading of TRANSCENDENCE, our
knowledge of the world, Sartre comes back to the definition
of knowledge, which, according to him, can be given only in
terms of being. Every knowledge, says Sartre, is intuitive;
deduction and discourse are means to reach an intuition. Intuition is defined by Husserl, and by most philosophers, as
the presence of the thing-in-itself to consciousness. But since
presence is an *"ek-static"* mode of being, we have to reverse
the terms and say that intuition is the presence of consciousness to being. To be present to something implies, as we have
seen, that one is not that something. The negation comes from

*standing
outside*

46

the being-for-itself. Knowledge, therefore, appears as a mode of *being*. Or, if one prefers, it is a certain way of *not being* a certain thing, which is at once posited as the non-self, or as *other*. (Consciousness, declares Hegel, distinguishes itself from something to which, at the same time, it relates itself.)

Knowledge is an internal negation.

We must, however, distinguish between external negation, by which we merely establish the exteriority of one thing to another—the tea cup is not the inkstand—and internal negation, in which the negated being qualifies the other by its absence from it. Only the being-for-itself can be affected thus by what it is not. The tea cup is not affected by the fact that it is not the inkstand; the distinction is established from outside and does not modify the nature of each. But when I say: "I am not rich," or, "I am not beautiful," I determine myself by these negative qualities which may explain part of my behavior.

In knowledge, consciousness, which is absolute nothingness, makes itself present to a particular object which it is not, thereby becoming a particular, or qualified, nothingness. The presence of consciousness to the object causes the object to become present to consciousness and to stand out against the nothingness of consciousness.

Fundamentally, knowledge is an internal negation. It causes itself to be qualified by that which it is not. In a sense, consciousness must *be* the object in order to deny that it is. When I look at that picture on the wall, my consciousness is there, with it, in fact it is nothing else than the picture. The

47

picture *is* really there, but of my consciousness all I can say is that it *is not* picture. As consciousness, I merely am the non-being which brings itself to existence from the fullness-of-being of the picture. As Husserl pointed out, consciousness has no contents, even in a degraded form; it merely aims at things, it is empty and intentional. Any consciousness must be consciousness of something; that something is the concrete pole of knowledge. In the rapport between the for-itself and the in-itself, the other pole is the nothingness of consciousness on which the object stands out. This nothingness, however, is a nothingness particularized, a particular nothing; and if we wonder how one nothing can differ from another, let us remember that language has one word to express the nothingness which results from the absence of things (nothing), and another for the nothingness which results from the absence of persons (nobody). Consciousness, as absolute nothingness, *becomes a particular nothingness as it makes itself present to a particular object, and* brings it to existence as being *there,* i.e., as a *presence.*

see p.10

This phenomenon appears in its purest form in fascination. *When the fascinating object is the world, we have an illusion of pantheistic fusion with the world.*

A psychological illustration of this phenomenon is found in fascination. In fascination the knower fully realizes his absolute nothingness as he faces the known. He does not identify himself with the fascinating object, yet he realizes that he is, literally, *nothing else.* The fascinating object is, so to speak, like a gigantic object in a deserted world. If fascination is exercised, not by a particular object, but by an intuition of presence to the world, it may bring about the illusion of a fusion of our consciousness with the world. This illusion is the basis of the pantheistic intuitions described by Rousseau and the romanticists. It did not mean fusion with the world, as they believed, but presence to it in a generalized form. In this presence to the world as a totality, consciousness is not the world, it is absolute nothingness, absolute negation, and it is this absolute negation of self which causes the world to surge as a totality.

The relation between being-in-itself and being-for-itself is neither continuity nor discontinuity; it is "identity denied."

Sartre's ontology constitutes, therefore, an absolute denial of the continuity which the romanticists, the Bergsonians, establish between the self and the cosmos. If there is identity between the two, it is an identity denied. To those who still think in terms of "life force" or *l'élan vital,* on the biological plane, Sartre's position would seem clearer at times if they were allowed to identify the being-in-itself with the unconscious forces of life; but his method is strictly to remain on the plane of phenomenology and to derive his ontology from the very structure of consciousness. To explain how the presence of the for-itself to the in-itself can be defined neither as continuity nor as discontinuity, he uses the image of two curbs tangent to each other: at the point where they meet, nothing separates them, they seem identical, but if we look at the two curbs in their entirety and reconstitute in our mind the movement which traced them, each one becomes, on the point where they meet, the negation of the other. There is no distance, no discontinuity between the two curbs at that point, yet they are distinct because the movement which traced one negates, as it were, the movement which traced the other.

Thus with the immediacy of the known in relation to the knower. Knowledge, as pure negativity, adds nothing to the known; it reveals it as *being there*. Conversely, while consciousness reveals the objects as extended, it apprehends its own non-extension, which is not a positive spiritual quality, but the negation of extension. This internal negation, which reveals being, is *"ek-static"* in character; it is what Sartre calls "transcendence."

2. Determination as negation.

Internal negation is an absolute. As the whole of negation, it is negation of the whole, and causes the world to surge as a totality against a background of non-being.

The original negation is a radical negation; as the whole of negation, the for-itself is negation of the whole. As a totality of negation, the for-itself confers totality on being and reveals "the world," which appears to consciousness as surrounded by nothingness; but this nothingness is merely the non-being of consciousness, which, through its transcendence, appears to itself as outside of being, excluded from the world. It is that non-being which limits the world and makes it a totality.

Consciousness is a totality, but it is a detotalized totality. Through external negation, it isolates the this *or the* that *from the background of undifferentiated totality of which it is internal negation. This passage from the continuity of the background to the discontinuity of the* this *and* that *constitutes space.*

But if consciousness is, or has to be, its own totality as negation, it can only be that totality in a detotalized form; on

50

the background of an undifferentiated totality of negation, consciousness negates itself as partial structure of the whole of being. "The being which I *am not* presently, inasmuch as it appears on the background of the totality of being, is the *this*." [48] The Gestalt theory brought to light this relation between the part and the whole, between "form" and "background." The "this" always appears on a background, i.e., on an undifferentiated totality of being negated by consciousness. As soon as another "this" appears, it may fuse with the background again. We might wonder at this point how a particular negation can stand out on the background of a totality of negation. The "this" stands out from its background because it is isolated by external negation, as not being the background. Since it is always possible to make a new *this* from the background and merge into it again, the background has an evanescent quality: "It is precisely this perpetual evanescence of the totality into a collection, of continuity into discontinuity, that one calls *space*." Space is a rapport established between beings which have no rapport by a being (consciousness) which is at once present to the totality of being and to the *this;* it is pure exteriority. It is neither the form nor the background; it is, rather, the possibility of the background to disintegrate into a multiplicity of forms for consciousness.

Determination springs from negation.

This pure exteriority is a non-being, a nothingness:

It is indeed because the inkstand is not the table—nor the pipe, nor the glass, etc.—that we can seize it as an inkstand. And yet, if I say: the inkstand is not the table, I think *nothing.*[49]

51

Determination, then, is indeed negation, according to the celebrated statement of Spinoza, but it is an ideal negation, patterned after the original negation.

3. Quality and quantity.

Just as consciousness stands before the object as not being the object, it stands before a certain aspect of the object (quality) as not being it.

To determine its non-being fully, consciousness not only has to negate that it is Being as a totality, and *this* being in particular, it also has to qualify itself as a certain way of not being this being. This determination corresponds to the determination of quality as a profile of the *this,* and belongs to the liberty of the for-itself. Quality is not an exterior aspect of being, it *is* being. The interpenetration of all the qualities of the object constitutes the object. The acidity of the lemon, its yellow color, are not merely superficial qualities of an empty form which would be the lemon, they are the lemon. To perceive the yellow color of the lemon is for consciousness to reflect itself as not being that quality.

I may "abstract" quality, but only as a certain way of being, which is for me a future possibility.

Quality, then, is being, but seen as one of its "profiles." I may, it is true, make an abstraction out of a certain quality; but as one of my future possibilities. How quality may suggest a certain mode of being, Sartre does not explain at this point. Suffice it to state that the abstract is, as one of my possibilities, the thing to come. This implies, as we shall see, belief in a

52

sort of universal existential symbolism which causes us to seek in the qualities of things the suggestion of a future way of being for ourselves; thus, for instance, the restlessness of the sea may reveal to the future navigator the possibility of a restless existence as his own possibility.

Quantity is the objectification of external negation. It is ideal, insofar as it is a rapport established by consciousness; it is in itself insofar as it expresses the indifference of being.

As to quantity, it is pure exteriority, ideal, yet objectified as if it were a thing-in-itself. The separation I introduce between things is ideal: I alone am conscious of it. Yet it is also in-itself, inasmuch as it is expressive of the independence of things. As I isolate my room from the rest of the world, which vanishes into the background, as I make myself present to that room, projecting upon it, as it were, a unity which is the unity of my self in order to think of it as *a* room, the objects in the room appear to me distinct and indifferent on the background of that unity. They appear distinct because I can make myself present to each object in turn by directing my attention upon them. My room is at once unity and multiplicity, but it could not be a multiplicity of objects if I had not conferred unity on it in the first place. *This* table and *that* chair belong to the same room. The conjunction "and" expresses an external negation: the table is not the chair, it merely expresses my realization that being-in-itself is what it is and nothing else. In itself, the conjunction is nothing, it is a nothing in itself, a nothing objectified by consciousness, it is *quantity*. If I add up the objects I see in the room, the number I obtain belongs neither to each individual object nor to their totality. Thus, space and quantity fundamentally represent the same type of negation: "they merely indicate the infinite diversity of the ways in which the liberty of the for-itself can realize the indifference of being."[50]

4. Potentiality and utensility.

In correlation with my possibilities, I confer on the things of the world potentialities such as permanence, probabilities, etc.

Being-for-itself, as internal negation of being-in-itself, projects to realize itself as presence to a future being. This is why the object reveals itself as endowed with potentialities varying from permanence to probabilities. These potentialities have their sense in the future and it is the for-itself which confers them. This landscape, for instance, made upon me an impression of quiet or wild beauty, which made me conscious of the fact that this sort of beauty was precisely what I lacked. I plan to recapture that impression by coming back to it, and in so doing I confer on the landscape either the character of permanence or, at least, the probability that it will retain the same character. This character, which I have abstracted from the landscape, is now *for me* a theme, an essence: quiet or wild beauty. When I face it again, in the same landscape, or anywhere else, it will still be with the same yearning, but this time it will be a gratified yearning. Essence will coincide with existence instead of following existence. We all know how fragile such a realization is outside of the level of art, which is the domain of the imaginary. If I am an artist, I shall try to evoke at once my yearning and its gratification through a painting and thus bring essence to coincide with existence. The beautiful is this coincidence which haunts the world as an unattainable value.

54

I also confer on them utensility. The order of utensils in the world is the image of my possibilities.

Unreflectively, I am not aware of the fact that I will always separate myself from what I am, but only of the incompleteness of things. I must therefore keep trying to reach my self through the world, and this is what Sartre calls "the circuit of ipseity." My own future is tied up with the future of the world, which appears to me as a complex of things and tools. Each thing of the world is at the same time a utensil which indicates my possibilities, and "as I *am* my possibilities, the order of utensils in the world is the image, projected into the in-itself, of my possibilities, i.e., of what I am." [51] The world, as complex of tool-things which reveals my possibilities, between my past and my future self, within the "circuit of ipseity," or selfness, is therefore a world of tasks in which I find myself engaged through the fact that any future is the future of a certain present and that, as consciousness, I am present to the world. It is an image of my self, since I am my possibilities, but that image is projected into the in-itself since it appears to me as a future state of the world. Heidegger errs when he states that the complex of tool-objects merely points to the realization of the for-itself.

The tool-objects of the world show the way to the realization of the self, not as absolute negation, but as realization of a self qualified by a past which it has to assume.

Why it should be so, why things appear as tools, indicating tasks to be accomplished, why consciousness is not content to remain as a mere negation of *this* and *that,* remains to be explained. Consciousness is not merely its future possibilities; it is also its past, or has to be its past. The self has to disperse itself on its three temporal dimensions. It has to seek the sense of its past in its future, but it also has to be its future within the perspective of a certain past. As I separate myself from the past, I become not a pure negation, but the negation of that past, a qualified negation. The sense of that negation is in my past consciousness, which now stands out in bold relief from among other things and other facts of the world. This past which is now a mere datum, a thing-in-itself, and as such my only concrete reality, I must save by grounding it in consciousness, by giving it meaning:

> The future is the past transcended (*le passé dépassé* as a given in-itself, toward an in-itself which would be its own foundation, i.e., which would be insofar as I would have to be it. My possible is the free resumption of that past insofar as that resumption can save it by giving it a foundation.[52]

5. World time.

The idea of universal time results from the projection of temporality into being.

Throughout his analysis of "being-in-the-world" as transcendence, Sartre made various allusions to past and future states of the world. We should realize, however, that the idea of a universal time is a spurious idea resulting from the projection of original temporality, which is the very structure of consciousness, on a static or moving world of being. Unreflectively, I am not conscious of my temporality; I discover it outside of consciousness, reflected by the world. Hence, the conception of a universal temporality, which is a sort of objective temporality.

Insofar as they appear to me as permanent, objects appear with a future and with a past. Change appears to me as causality. As an object changes, I conceive of the change as absolute dispersion of instants exterior to each other, within the unity of Time which is necessity. This conception contains a contradiction.

As I perceive the things of the world, I confer on them at once the three dimensions of my temporality. This inkstand in front of me appears to me with a future and with a past, i.e., with a character of permanence. In the future, it appears to me as the idea of an inkstand, i.e., as an essence in the past, as a co-presence to my own presence; and since my past presence to the inkstand is now objectified and in itself, there is really no difference between the past of the inkstand and my own, except that I *have to* assume my past. If objects are not perceived as permanent, but as coming into being and being replaced by others, I establish between objects a cause and effect relationship. Thus external temporality appears to me as absolute dispersion within a unity which is Time. Each "before" and each "after" appears as an instant exterior to other instants, yet all these instants merge within the unity of a single being which is Time. Time is dispersion conceived as necessity.

This contradiction is due to the fact that world time appears on the double foundation of consciousness and of being.

The contradictory nature of time, as it appears to us, i.e., a unity and multiplicity at once, is due to the fact that it appears on the double foundation of the for-itself and of the in-itself, of consciousness and of being. Outside of consciousness, being is what it is. The idea of change, with a "before" and an "after," comes from consciousness. What the foundation of that idea is *in being* is a metaphysical question outside of ontology, as Sartre understands it.

The present is presence of consciousness to being. Presence of consciousness to a motionless object reveals the ek-*static movement by which consciousness makes itself present to being.*

The preceding considerations apply primarily to the past of the world. The present reveals being to consciousness as motionless or in motion. If the object revealed to the presence of consciousness is motionless, it is simply perceived as being and as having been in the past, identical with itself. It is more difficult to point out what, in motion, comes from being and what comes from consciousness. In motion, the object can no longer be defined by its relations of pure exteriority with other objects. If it becomes exterior to its exteriority, it is exterior to itself. Its manner of being has changed. It remains in suspense between abolishment and permanence. Through motion, consciousness discovers its own exteriority-to-itself. The trajectory reveals that exteriority within the unity of a single being. When the *this* is at rest, space *is;* when it is in motion, space is engendered, and is engendered in time. Sartre's description of motion is not intended as a metaphysical explanation. It merely points out how, through motion, consciousness receives the revelation of its own exteriority to self, as a mere presence to that which it is not. Motion is a perfect symbol of its perpetual flight. We ask motion for the realization of universal time because the present of the mobile object announces to consciousness its own presence as exteriority to self, with, of course, this difference: consciousness has to assume the being to which it is exterior.

The original future is the gamut of my potentialities. These are related by me to future states of the world.

The original future of consciousness is the possibility of its presence to a being-in-itself beyond the real being-in-itself. My future, therefore, implies a future world and is directly connected with the real to which I am present, since it is only my possibility to modify the present. Thus my future is made up of a gamut of potentialities: permanence, essences, powers. There is, then, a universal future. It appears to me in the essences of things, because, as soon as I determine the essence of something I am already in the future; thus, the permanence and utensility of the table refer to my future use of the table. A future of the world may be defined as a chance, a probability, etc. Each *this* has a future of this sort.

The universal future is an abstract frame containing all my potentialities as reflected on the things of this world. Its cohesion is a reflection of the unity of consciousness.

The universal future is obviously an abstract frame which we conceive of as containing the whole hierarchy of all futures. We conceive these futures as exterior to each other within a frame exterior to them. Closely considered, its cohesion crumbles down into a multiplicity of instants which, considered in turn, lose their temporal nature. That cohesion is nothing but a reflection of the for-itself seeking its self. Time has no being except in the act through which we give it reality by extending it, like a bridge, toward the realization of a project. We conceive it mostly as *lapse,* and a lapse of time is the ideal distance which separates me from myself. Within that lapse, I compress a series of possibilities related to my major project, and so time appears to me as an objective temporal form which is like the trajectory of my act.

6. Knowledge of the world.

Knowledge can be defined in terms of being: it is only the presence of the in-itself to the for-itself.

Knowledge is only the presence of being to the for-itself, and *there is* being only because the for-itself negates itself. As it negates itself, it becomes affirmation of the in-itself. There is nothing outside of what I see, or could see. Space, time, utensility are mere conditions of the realization of being through internal negation by the for-itself. Yet space, time, and utensility separate me radically from being. When the for-itself affirms that it knows being "such as it is," it affirms its non-being, it places itself outside of being. The for-itself is immediate presence to being and at the same time there is an infinite distance between being-in-itself and being-for-itself. That is because the ideal of knowledge is being-what-one-knows, and its original structure, not-being-what-one-knows:

> . . . knowledge, intermediary between being and non-being, refers me to absolute being if I want it (to be) subjective, and refers me to myself when I think I am grasping the absolute. The very sense of knowledge is what it is not and is not what it is, for to know a being such as it is, one would have to be that being, but there is a "such as it is" only because I am not the being that I know, and if I be-

60

came that being, the "such as it is" would vanish and could not even be thought . . . Knowledge places us in the presence of the absolute, and there is a truth of knowledge. But that truth, although it delivers us nothing more or less than the absolute, remains strictly human.[53]

The body appears not as knowing but as known, and known primarily by others.

No mention has been made so far of the senses and of the part played by the body in the process of knowing. This is because the body appears primarily as known, and not as knowing. Furthermore, it is primarily known by *others,* and what we *know* of our body, we know through our knowledge of the other's body, and through his knowledge of our body. As I discover my body, I discover another mode of existence as fundamental as being-for-itself: *being-for-others.*

61

IV   Being-For-Others

1. The problem of the other's existence.

Both the realist and the idealist conceive my relation with the other as external negation.

Sartre rejects both the idealist and the realist points of view in regard to the existence of others:

> At the origin of the problem of the existence of others, there is a fundamental presupposition: my fellowman (*autrui*) is *the other*, i.e., the Ego which *is not* my Ego, (*le moi qui n'est pas moi*); we therefore detect a negation as the constitutive structure of being-the-other (*l'être-autrui*). The presupposition common to idealism and realism is that the constituting negation is one of exteriority.[54]

This is because the other appears to me through the perception of a body. The realist sees himself separated from the other as a chair is separated from the table: in space. The idealist may reduce both his body and the body of the other to objective systems of representation, but in idealism each consciousness remains exterior to the other consciousness, since each one is a complete system of representation. Each subject is limited by itself only: the world is *my* representation. This type of separation is a kind of exteriority in space. Moreover, the idealist is unaware that this conception presupposes a "third man" to establish this relationship. This witness may take the form of God, who at once is his creatures, since he creates them, and is not his creatures since he is their witness; a relationship expressed by the conception of creation. But this conception raises new problems, as is shown by post-Cartesian thought. If creation is *continued,* I am in suspense between a distinct existence and pantheistic fusion with the creator. If creation is an original act and if I have become a closed system within my own consciousness, God knows me as exterior to himself, in the way a sculptor knows his work: as an object. The notion of God, while revealing interior negation as the only possible connection between various consciousness, remains ineffective.

In Husserl, the presence of tool-things in the world refers to the existence of the other. The existence of the other is as sure as that of the world but no more.

Since the 18th century, philosophy has been trying to eliminate the gap between my consciousness and the consciousness of the other by considering them otherwise than two separate substances. The connection has been sought in the very structure of consciousness; but by seeking that connection in *knowledge,* modern philosophy still maintains exteriority—external negation—as the link between my consciousness and the other's. In Husserl, the objects of the world refer, as tools, to the existence of others. Whether I consider this table or that tree in solitude or in company, the others are still there with all the meanings which are attached to the table or to the tree, which constitute the table or the tree. Their existence is as sure as the existence of the world; the solipsist might answer: "Yes, but no more." Husserl himself admitted that when my consciousness aims at the other (the other's consciousness), it discovers the other as an absence.

In Hegel, the existence of the other as consciousness is proven by the fact that I need his recognition to establish the identity of my own. A consciousness, however, cannot recognize another as such except in an objectified form.

In his *Phenomenology of the Mind,* a work from which Sartre seems to have derived more than one suggestion, Hegel has offered a more satisfactory explanation. Self-consciousness is identical with itself through the exclusion of every other consciousness. That exclusion constitutes implicit recognition. Hegel places himself on the plane of reciprocal relations between one consciousness and the other, which Descartes does not, since by saying: "I think, therefore I am," he already takes himself for granted. Through the *cogito,* I appear to myself as an individuality; I apprehend myself as an object, on the reflective plane, as distinct from the other, whose existence I thereby imply. Hegel's merit is to have pointed out that as a free consciousness I could not be an object for myself, and had to seek recognition of myself, as subject and as object, from a foreign consciousness. But I could not seek that recognition if I did not first recognize the other as subject. This is the basis of Hegel's famous explanation of the master to slave relationship: as subject, the other sees me objectively, bound to a body and immersed in the flux of life. To be recognized by the other as a free subject, as pure consciousness, I must prove that I am not bound to my body, I must risk my life, I must attack him. If the other is unwilling to take the same risk, he proves himself to be more attached to his body and to his life than I am. Hegel's merit here is to suggest that I am a being-for-itself which is for itself only for the other. But Hegel does not realize that if I become a subject for the other, he will become an object for me, and will be unable to recognize me. Hegel views all consciousness from the viewpoint of totality. By so doing he makes of the plurality of consciousnesses a plurality of objects, and of himself a sort of transcendental subject. He is still on the plane of knowledge. My relation with the other is a relation from being to being, not of knowledge to knowledge:

> for I can, no doubt, transcend myself *toward* the All, but I cannot establish myself within that All to contemplate myself and to contemplate others. No logical or epistemological optimism then could bring an end to the scandal of plurality of consciousnesses.[55]

To Heidegger, my relation with the other is being, not knowledge, being with, *not being* for. *My being* with *others in the world is as certain as the world, but no more. It neither makes solipsism impossible nor explains the dialectics of concrete relations between two individuals. The element of negation is absent in Heidegger's* Mitsein.

Heidegger, if he did not solve the problem, at least stated it properly by placing it, not on the plane of knowledge, but on the plane of *being.* Heidegger defines "human reality" as *being in* the world *with* other human beings. These modes of

65

being are inseparable from each other. For "human reality," being consists in finding itself in a finite world (*Dasein*) with other human beings (*Mitsein*). We ask the world, as the sum total of our possibilities, to reveal to us what we are; if we live an *authentic* life, all our actions are subordinated to the realization of our finitude between birth and death; our birth, of course, is a contingent circumstance, but in a movement of transcendence toward our authentic self, we can give sense to our death, which is our most authentic possibility. I am not alone in this movement of transcendence. I am in it with others, and inasmuch as they share that movement of transcendence through the world, they are in a sense part of me. In my unauthentic life with others, I accept the role of an interchangeable human being of the sort designated by the indefinite pronouns "one," "people," "they": to go from Columbus Circle to Grand Central, *one* must change trains at Times Square. This interchangeable human being is an abstraction, a pure non-being, a convenient myth, the impersonal entity aimed at by signs, taboos, and "How to Use" leaflets, to insure common discipline, or to offer guidance in the execution of impersonal tasks. Set up as an ideal, it does away with anguish, and through social conformism, small talk, curiosity and diversion, leads to the unauthentic life. The authentic *Mitsein* might be symbolized by the effort of the team to win the boat race. It is intimately felt in the common rhythm of the rowers; each one of them feels within himself the same movement of transcendence toward a common goal, on the horizon of a common world, and feels it *with* the other rowers. In this conception, however, being *for* others has been replaced by being *with* others. It reveals the coexistence of consciousnesses without explaining it. If you do away with the element of negation in the concept of the other, you identify individual consciousness with world consciousness, and you slip back into idealism, taking others along with you. You have not escaped solipsism.

To show that solipsism is impossible, I must show that my being for others is part of the cogito, *and is as certain as my existence.*

To escape from solipsism, I need no proof of the existence of others, I simply must demonstrate that solipsism is impossible, as I implicitly and unreflectively acknowledge in daily life. I must go back to the pre-reflective *cogito,* and see whether it will not reveal me the existence of others in the same concrete way as it has already revealed me the existence of the thing-in-itself: through negation. If the other, however, is to appear to me as a consciousness, the negation must be internal, not external, since I also am a consciousness, and in that case the multiplicity of consciousnesses must be a totality, as Hegel claimed; but the nature of that totality must be such as to make it impossible to adopt the point of view of totality. It must be a detotalized totality, since each one is conscious of being himself insofar as he is not the other.

2. Concrete realization of the other as consciousness.

The existence of the other as subject is concretely revealed to me when I feel myself becoming an object for him under his glance.

If I am alone in the park, the landscape seems organized around me; every distance can be measured from the place where I stand, things have distinct qualities for me, I am the center of reference of the world about me. Other people may appear in the distance. They figure as accessories, may even add a picturesque note as do the characters which the painter fits into his composition. If one of them becomes aware of my presence, comes toward me and looks at me, the situation is suddenly altered. Another frame of reference has surged within my own world, distances are now measured from another person, another world has been superimposed on mine and I figure in it, in my turn, as an accessory, as an object. In a flash, my universe disintegrates and is flushed away from me. I now exist in the universe of another, at a given distance from the person who constitutes the center of that universe. The change came through the fact that I am now being looked at. When I am looked at, I no longer perceive the shape or color of the eyes fixed on me, I am referred to my own self. If I do see their shape or color, I cease perceiving the look. This is so true that I do not even have to see eyes peering at me to have the sensation of being looked at. In hostile territory, human glances lurk behind every bush. Being seen, then, primarily means that I no longer am the observer who determines the frame of reference of my world. My being-in-the-world and my being-for-myself are at once affected. Under the look of the other, I realize that I figure in his world as an object, occupying a certain amount of space, within a given situation. Conversely, he is revealed to me as subject, as consciousness. The ridicule or the shame of a certain situation may be suddenly revealed to me as I discover that someone is looking at me. I discover myself then as existing for another, as object for his consciousness. Certain feelings have no other origin than my being-for-others, and I cannot think for a moment of denying them: I am this feeling of ridicule or that feeling of shame. The other, then, appears to me, not as an object in the world, but as a pure transcendence, as an intention, a transcendence and intention which are not mine; it reveals to me that, while I cannot be an object for myself, I can be an object for the other. The other separates himself from me in the same way as I separate myself from the in-itself. Yet there is a difference.

I become an object for the other inasmuch as I become for him a transcended-transcendence.

The object that I become under the look of the other is not of the type of the in-itself. I am still free, but my liberty has been circumscribed. My transcendence has become a pure datum. In the eyes of the other, I figure as limited transcendence. My possibilities have been turned into probabilities. My subjectivity has been objectified. In short, I am now a *transcended-transcendence.* A somewhat forceful image of what is meant here by "transcended transcendence" might be suggested by the flight of a fugitive from justice, trapped in a given area, darting in every possible direction toward every possible issue and discovering at every move that his *space,* as well as every *possibility* for escape, are thoroughly covered. Even if he could not see his pursuers, he would realize that their seeing him has alienated space for him: that space he is standing in is no longer his own.

My transcendence in time *as in* space *is modified by the* simultaneity *of another's transcendence.*

Awareness of the other also alienates time by giving it a new dimension: simultaneity. If I were alone in the world, my consciousness would only be presence to the world. The look of others reveals to me a co-presence which throws me into a universal present, and that universal present is an alienation of my own presence to the universe.

My objectivity for others stays with me, as part of me, in the absence of the other, which means the possibility of his presence. In an impersonal form, the presence of the other is referred to, even in his absence by the tool-things of the world.

The objectivity which the other confers on me is not, therefore, the being-in-itself which my consciousness at once negates and has to assume. It is I, but given another dimension and negated by *another* consciousness. Therefore, it escapes me. The meanness or the cowardliness that the other sees in me is not for me a full and complete intuition of what I am. Yet, although I would not think of myself as mean or cowardly but for the presence of others, I have to experience these modes of being at a distance from myself, in the minds of others. The other does not have to be present in person for me to feel his presence as subject. Let us say, for instance, that I am spying through a key-hole; I hear footsteps, think that I have been detected, and experience shame. It was a false alarm. I resume my position. Yet the shame may not disappear. Although I am sure that no one *is there,* yet the existence of the other as subject is still with me. A person may be said to be absent from a place only when that person *might* have been there. At the Café de Flore, known to be patronized by Sartre, one might perhaps say: "M. Sartre is absent," but one could not add: "and the Pope is absent, too," without passing from sense to nonsense. Thus can we say that there is "presence in absence." As a possible presence, the other is ubiquitous presence, even in absence. Moreover, there are all around me signs of his presence far more impressive than the human footprint on the sand of Robinson Crusoe's island. All the tool-things of the world, and their utensility, refer to that presence.

In that impersonal form, expressed by impersonal pronouns like one, they, people, I conceive the consciousness of others as a totality, corresponding to the notion of God.

If I try to abstractly construe this consciousness of others which encompasses my own, I only reach the concept of an omnipresent and infinite subject, corresponding to the notion of God. It is only when I look at others, and objectify their subjectivity, that they become a multiplicity. If I talk to an audience, I experience the look of the audience as *a look,* even though I am not conscious of dealing with an integrated collective body. If I want to make sure that I am being understood, I look in turn at the audience and see individual heads and eyes appear. What I had experienced at first was an anonymous look corresponding to the impersonal pronoun: *one.* This impersonal *one* is always with me: It is my being-for-others, quite distinct from my being-for-itself.

I objectify the other through internal negation, *by denying that I am the other.*

The nature of that distinction is internal negation. It is essentially the same as the distinction between being-for-itself and being-in-itself. If *there is* another, it is because I am not that other, because I distinguish myself from him. This negation at once affirms my being as an individual and the being of the other, and I *am* that negation, spontaneously and con-

71

tinuously. In fact, as self-consciousness, I am nothing more than my negation of being the other, in the same way as my consciousness of the chair apprehends itself as *not being* the chair.

Conversely, the other is he for whom my for-itself is objectively, but I cannot retain this objectivity without losing my own subjectivity. If I affirm my subjectivity, he, in turn, becomes an object for me. As this process confirms our separation, I negate the negation by which the other made me an object: I reject myself rejected. Through this limitation, my consciousness becomes a detotalized totality.

Yet there is a difference. In this case the negation is reciprocal. The other is also a consciousness, with possibilities which are not my own. His consciousness negates being my consciousness and it must, therefore, recognize my being-for-itself in order to refuse it. Thus my consciousness becomes object for his consciousness, which it cannot be for mine. The other, as subject, possesses a dimension of my being which is inaccessible to me. The other is he-for-whom-my-for-itself is. If, however, I accept being an object in the other's subjectivity, I lose my own subjectivity; I cease being a *transcending*-transcendence and become a *transcendent*-transcendence. If, on the other hand, I affirm my subjectivity by making the other an object, a transcended-transcendence in his turn, I lose my own objectivity. In order to retain my subjectivity, I finally have to reject this objectivity which the other's consciousness confers on my own by distinguishing itself from mine. I reject myself rejected. But as I tear myself from the other, leaving my alienated self in his hands, I recognize at once the existence of the other and of my objective being-for-others.

72

This acceptance, in refusal, of my alienated self is at once my bond with others and the symbol of our absolute separation. It is not given once and for all, even though we may try to consider it that way by saying: "Let the others think of me what they like." It has to be freely and perpetually reassumed, and this is the price we pay for not falling into voluntary solipsism. It is a limitation, inasmuch as consciousness can be limited only by consciousness. As consciousness, I am a totality; as a consciousness limited by a foreign consciousness, I am a detotalized totality. The other appears first to me as a transcendence which limits my own. I grasp first that negation for which I am not responsible, but as I grasp that negation of myself, I realize that I am responsible for a negation of the other which is my own possibility, I discover my self as negation of the other. Thus by assuming the limitation conferred on me by the other, I turn it into a mere datum and confer on the other the limitation which defines him as "other."

Shame is the sense of that limitation in its original form. One may experience shame either before the other individualized, or before the other depersonalized. Posited as the subject which cannot be made object, the other depersonalized is conceived as God.

The various attitudes we may assume toward the other confirm this situation. Shame is the original recognition of the limitation which the existence of the other imposes upon my consciousness. It is the feeling of the original fall in its purest form. I see myself fallen among the things of the world, as a kind of object. The shame experienced on being seen nude is its symbolic form. To dress is to claim the privilege of seeing without being seen, like a pure subject. Thus did Adam and Eve, in the symbolic language of Genesis, know after the fall that they were nude. The natural reaction of defense against such a feeling is to consider the other as an object in his turn. By so doing we do not deny his subjectivity, but the other appears as having an outside as well as an inside. He is like a camera which may register images of me which I can modify. His transcendence has acquired a character of "interiority." The other, however, may be perceived in his depersonalized form as well as in his individualized form. In that case we refer to him as "one," "they," "people." If we posit the depersonalized other as the subject which cannot be realized as object, this form becomes God before whom I posit, in turn, the eternity of the object which I am for his consciousness. Black magic represents an effort to reverse the process and to confer on God the character of an object. It is an attempt to transcend divine transcendence by going directly against God's will; but such an attempt implies recognition of God as the absolute subject which cannot be made object, and contains implicit contradiction.

Self-respect means free assumption of that limitation and a sense of responsibility toward the alienated self. Vanity is an attempt to use the subjectivity of others to confer objectivity to our qualities. Pride is the assumption of our subjectivity.

Self-respect, pride, vanity are variations on the theme of shame. Self-respect acknowledges the objectivity of consciousness for others, holds itself responsible for it, and assumes that responsibility. The self-respecting man tries to affect the other without ceasing to be an object for him; the object of his respect. The same is true of vanity. In vanity, I try, through

74

a foreign consciousness, to confer objectivity on some of my qualities. In so doing, I use the other's consciousness as a means to an end, as an object, which of course implies contradiction and brings ridicule instead of admiration. Pride is the sense of my subjectivity. Only shame and pride are authentic feelings, being respectively the original sense of our objectivity and the affirmation of our subjectivity before the other.

3. The other as object.

The other as object is a transcended-transcendence. As transcendence, he is committed to certain tasks but I do not perceive him as committing himself; his subjectivity appears as an absence.

Self-respect, vanity, pride are various ways of apprehending one's subjectivity, thereby objectifying the other's in various degrees. Becoming aware of my self, I cause the other to exist as an object in my world. Not that I deny completely his transcendence as "other." I recognize it, not as a *transcending-transcendence* but as a *transcended-transcendence*. The other still appears to me as committed to certain tasks, but this commitment assumes a character of passivity. He is committed in the same way as a policy is committed to writing. His commitment is, as it were, written on the surface of the tool-things of the world, but his subjectivity appears to me as an absence.

Objectified, the depersonalized Other appears as objective totality. This totality is the background on which the other

75

*appears as a particular object. The other as object is an auton-
omous center of reference within my world.*

If, in reaction to my intuition of the other-subject in depersonalized form, as a totality, I try to objectify his subjectivity,
I apprehend him as objective totality coextensive with the
totality of the world. On the background of this objective
totality, the other appears as a form, just as an object of this
world appears as a *this* on the background of a totality of
objects. As I look at this angry man in the street, I perceive
a red face, cries, and threatening gestures; these signs do not
refer to subjective anger, they refer to other similar incidents.
Is the angry man going to strike? I can only judge this situation
and assess its probabilities in terms of other similar situations. This does not mean that the behaviorists are right in
interpreting man in terms of situations; the other is a transcended-transcendence, which means that to understand him
we must understand his goals. But even if we reverse the be-
haviorist viewpoint, the objectivity of the other will remain
intact:

> for what is primarily objective—whether we call it *significa-
> tion,* after the style of French or British psychologists, *in-
> tention* after the style of phenomenologists, *transcendence*
> like Heidegger, or *form* like the Gestaltists—it is the fact
> that the Other cannot be defined otherwise than by a
> totalitarian organization of the world and that he is the
> key to that organization.[56]

The Other objectified is an autonomous center of reference
within my world. Fear of the enemy, even objectified, does
not consist merely of a few gestures, of a fall on rocky ground.
It is a complete change in the organization of the world. The
deserting soldier, as he throws away his gun, and turns toward

his rear lines, has seen his horizon closed by the enemy as by a wall, and now his horizon opens up back of him as a refuge. I can grasp the whole situation without ceasing to see the soldier objectively.

My relations with the other tends primarily to make him stay as object for me.

My apprehension of the other is then, first of all, that of a subjective totality, then that of a concrete subject which I cannot limit as particular subject, then, in defensive reaction, of a particular object on the background of a degraded objective totality. But the other can always reassume his subjectivity:

> My constant care then is to contain the other within his objectivity, and my relations with the other as object are made up essentially of ruses intended to make him stay an object.[57]

Since a single look from the other suffices to render all my precautions useless, I am thrown back and forth from the feeling of my subjectivity to that of my objectivity, without ever being able to conciliate these two modes of being.

4. Metaphysical aspect of the question.

Being-for-others seems to be the third attempt of being to tear itself from its contingency. Everything happens as if a totality of for-itself was trying to ground itself in being.

Sartre, at this point, is tempted to raise the same question as the hero of Huxley's *Eyeless in Gaza*: "Why are there

77

others?" Everything happens, in a way, as if my consciousness and the consciousness of the other were the same originally. Summing up the foregoing, we realize that being-for-others constitutes the third attempt of being-in-itself to tear itself from its contingency, or, to use Sartre's expression, its third "*ek-stasy.*" The first was the three-dimensional project of being-for-itself, negating its being-in-itself and assuming it at the same time, in the light of the future. The second was that of the reflective for-itself to *be* that negation as for-itself-in-itself, and to confer on it a sort of objectivity. The third is that of being-for-others. In this case, as in the other two, the negation is internal but this time it is reciprocal. For me to be able to negate that I am the other, it must be that there is a being which is at once my self and the other self. Hegel seems to be right: "it is the point of view of the totality which is the point of view of being, the true point of view":

> Everything happens as if the others and myself were marking the vain effort of a totality of being-for-itself to get hold of itself again and to envelop what it *has to be* on the pure and simple mode of the in-itself.[58]

Yet, through simultaneous negation, consciousnesses affirm themselves as incompatible absolutes.

On the other hand, my negation of myself operates simultaneously with the other's negation that he is me, and without these two negations, there could be no being-for-others. It seems as if a pure non-being had slipped into a totality of consciousness to break it up, "as non-being, in Leucippus' atomism, slips into the Parmenidean totality of being to shatter it into atoms."[59] Yet that non-being does not appear as the foundation of the multiplicity of consciousnesses, for, again,

78

if it were, there could be no being-for-others, except merely as the expression of that multiplicity.

On the metaphysical plane, being-for-others points to an original totality of Mind. Starting from the fact of the plurality of consciousnesses, we must face it as pure contingency.

Thus we reach a contradictory conclusion: being-for-others can be only through a totality which undoes itself so that it may be. But, on the other hand, being-for-others can exist only through a separateness which no totality, even the totality of Mind, can produce. In a sense, the metaphysical sense, the multiplicity of consciousnesses refers us to an original totality of Mind tearing itself apart; in another sense, if we start from the fact of plurality, the metaphysical question loses all meaning, and that plurality appears as pure contingency. It is so because it is so. "The *ek-static* totality of Mind is not simply a detotalized totality, but it appears to us as a broken-up being of which one can neither say that it exists nor that it does not." [60] And so, adds Sartre, "the multiplicity of consciousnesses appears to us as a *synthesis* and not as a *collection;* but it is a synthesis the totality of which is inconceivable." [61]

The other's objectivity is made manifest by his body.

We discovered that the existence of the other as subject was made evident to us through the experience of our objectivity for him; that the reaction to that experience was our apprehension of the other as object. Briefly, the other can exist for us in two ways: if I experience his subjective being with evidence, I fail to know him; if I know him and act on him,

79

I reach only his objective being and the probability of his existence. That object which the other is for me is made manifest by his body.

5. The three ontological dimensions of the body.

As the other's objectivity is made manifest through his body, I tend to know the human body as the other's body, even my own.

When I think of the human body, I think primarily of the body of others, objectively. I do so even when I am looking at an X-ray of my own. It is a thing among the things of the world. If I look at my hand, it is an object like any other object, at a certain distance from my eyes, as is my typewriter. But my body can also be, unreflectively, that which reveals to me the things of the world, in which case I no longer think of it nor see it. When my hand reveals to me the surface and resistance of things, I am merely conscious of the things my hand feels. There are, therefore, two ways to experience the existence of our body; objectively and subjectively, as being-for-others and as being-for-itself. We should, however, reverse this order if we wish to describe what the body is for us on the unreflective plane before we define its existence as known.

I experience the existence of my body unreflectedly either as the condition of my transcendence or as pure contingence. As the condition of my transcendence, it is the unseen center of reference toward which the tool-things of the world are pointing. As contingence, the existence of my body is revealed to me directly through nausea.

80

On the plane of the for-itself, the body could be defined as the contingent form assumed by the necessity of my contingency. It is not an in-itself within the for-itself; it *is* the for-itself inasmuch as the for-itself is not its own foundation but has to exist as a contingent being among other contingent beings, here and now. As such, it cannot be distinguished from the situation of the for-itself. In every perception, there is an element of necessity, an element of contingency, and an element of freedom: the book must appear to me either on the right or on the left of the table, it is contingent on my position that it should appear on the left rather than on the right, and I am free to look at the book rather than at the table. My whole field of vision refers to a center of reference which I *am*, and cannot see. The orientation of things within that field of vision refers to a certain order which I have introduced into things through the mere contingent fact of my existence among them. The world refers to my bodily presence as a center of reference. If I lose the sense of sight, objects still exist for me but without the center of reference of a visible totality. Thus, it is the surge of the for-itself in the world which brings about at once the emergence of the world, as a totality of things and of the senses. The body is my engagement individualized, and Plato was not wrong to present the body as that which individualizes the soul; but, on the other hand, the soul is the body inasmuch as the for-itself is *its* own individualization. We must conclude that the body is the primary condition of my transcendence as well as the contingent structure of my being. As my contingency, my body is *for me* my birth, my past, the necessity of a point of view. Yet my liberty is inconceivable outside of that contingency. By the very fact that I live, I have accepted my body and its infirmities, together with my finitude; but it is up to me to assume these infirmities as "to be proud of," "to be suppressed," or "to be tolerated." When we say that the body is the condition of our transcendence, we do not mean that it is just a tool among other tools for consciousness; we mean consciousness transcends the body as one transcends the sign toward its signification. In this process, the body becomes "the neglected one" but consciousness still *is* the body inasmuch as it is nothing else but a qualified internal negation. The contingency of which the body is a sign is revealed to us in pain. When I read, if I cease transcending letters, words and lines toward their meaning, my eyes will begin to hurt as the characters become blurred and dance before my eyes, and I will become conscious of a certain pain which is in proportion to the degree my attention is turned away from that which I am reading. As pain progresses, I may try to view it objectively, on the reflective plane. I may even lend it a sort of magic life of its own, speak of my sickness as of some familiar visitor. As I project upon its variations the unity of original temporalization, I reach the concept of an interpenetration of states of consciousness which to Bergson is duration and liberty, and which to Sartre is just psychic duration. When it is not painful, non-positional consciousness of my contingency is revealed to me under the form of a discreet and unbearable nausea which is the root of physical nausea and is strictly of the same nature. In conclusion, my body appears to my consciousness either as the center of reference pointed to by the tool-objects of the world, or as the contingency which consciousness has to live down, and these two modes of being are complementary.

I experience the existence of the other's body *as that of a new center of reference which I can see and which is superimposed on mine. I transcend the other's transcendence through objective interpretation of his actions in a given situation; this leads to knowledge of character, which is transcended-transcendence. I may study objectively the reactions and structure of his body. This leads to the abstract notion of "life."*

This is what my body is for me, unreflectively. The other's body may also be apprehended unreflectively, as well as objectively known. The other is at first a new center of reference superimposed on mine, a transcendence which I must transcend; the tool-things of the world point to him as the new center of reference. Yet, while my own center of reference is a viewpoint on which there is no viewpoint, an empty center of reference, I can view the other's viewpoint as his body. I can even study that body objectively, merely as a body, and understand my "facticity" through his. Such is the object of physiology. The other's body, then, is primarily the facticity of a transcended-transcendence, a facticity which refers to my own. There are even moments when I lose sight of the transcendence, and when the other's body appears to me as pure contingency. It is then perceived by me as flesh and I experience something similar to the nausea which is like the taste of my own contingency. Generally, the other's body appears to me within a situation, with a signification: I see him walking, sitting down to read, working, etc. The totality of these significations corresponds to the notion of *life* which is therefore, in the abstract, transcended-transcendence, and life appears as the background on which I perceive this body or this organ. My perception of the other's body differs from my perception of things insofar as I perceive it on the background of a situation, and insofar as I do not perceive a particular organ except in relation to life. The meaning of gestures is somewhere outside, in space, and if Peter gets up suddenly, I look around to see where he is going. I relate the movement of the organ to the body as a whole. Hence the feeling of horror before a hand sticking out from a cavity, or creeping along the door frame. Character and temperament are other indications of the existence of the other as transcended-transcendence. We do not know our own character, and we know the character of the other only through external manifestations. As a matter of fact, it is nothing else but these manifestations. We grasp them as a synthetic ensemble before we analyze their structure. This does not mean that we implicitly believe in the fatality of character to the extent of denying the other any form of liberty. The other's liberty is just objectified liberty: knowing the other's tendency to become angry, I still consider him responsible for his anger, which is, for me, equally a part of his transcendence; but it is a transcendence which I can transcend and act upon in the present as I calm or provoke that anger, and take it into account as I project my own future.

I can also transfer the objectivity of the other's body to my own. The abstraction of language favors that process.

The human body, then, appears with different dimensions of being as *my* body and as *the other's* body; it appears with a third ontological dimension as *my* body *for others*. Through the look of the other, I am revealed to myself as object, insofar as I have become for him a transcended-transcendence. I do not know what kind of an object I have become for the other, but I feel responsible for it. I am responsible for being there and then, with a body. For the other, indeed, as we have seen, I am not merely a transcended-transcendence I am my factual existence, my facticity. My body, that unknowable instrument, is seen by the other, and, insofar as he transcends the possibilities which I try to make my own, through interpretation of my gestures, expressions, etc., that body appears to me as one of the tool-things of the world, within a frame of reference which is not mine. This is directly experienced in shyness. The shy person is "embarrassed by his body," or rather by the fact that while he simply experiences the existence of his body, the other sees it. His hands are there, limp by his sides, *for nothing,* a mere contingency. He will try to use them, like instruments, to convey the correct impression, but this is like a sort of blind fire of which the results cannot be verified. The existence of our body for others is as real to us as its existence for us. In fact, the other fulfils a function which we ourselves cannot fulfil: he sees us as we are. We become resigned to see ourselves through his eyes. Language permits us to do so on an abstract plane, and it is at that level that the assimilation of my body with the other's body takes place. The sick man knows his sickness through what the doctor tells him about it. It is still his sickness since he feels it, but it has an independent life of its own which the doctor knows better than the patient. The doctor is responsible for it, and the patient's body becomes an object for the doctor. It is possible, therefore, to consider our body as existing for others. But this fact should not be made the starting point of a theory of knowledge concerning the body. Insofar as I can see parts of my body through a mere anatomical contingency, I may adopt, concerning them, the point of view of the other. Primarily, the body is the instrument which I *am.*

6. Concrete relations with others.

In dealing with others, we either try to confer objectivity on them so as to retain our subjectivity, or else we allow them to retain their subjectivity, and therefore their liberty, so as to obtain their free recognition of our own subjectivity.

My concrete relations with others depend on the attitude I adopt on discovering that I am an object for the other's subjectivity:

> I may . . . attempt, insofar as I am fleeing the in-itself which I am without grounding it, to deny that being which is conferred on me from outside; which means that I may turn to the other and confer objectivity on him in my turn, since the objectivity of the other does away with my objectivity for the other. But, on the other hand, inasmuch as the other as liberty is the foundation of my being-in-itself, I may seek to recuperate this liberty and to get hold of it without depriving it of its free character: if I could, indeed, assimilate this liberty which is the foundation of my being-in-itself, I should be, to myself, my own foundation.[62]

These two basic attitudes are opposed to each other, but the failure of one motivates the adoption of the other. The patterns of behavior through which the for-itself attempts to assimilate the other's liberty will, arbitrarily, be treated first.

This last resolve is the basis of love, language, and masochism. Through them, I respect the subjectivity of others so as to obtain recognition of my own. But the only way to preserve the subjectivity of others is to remain an object for them.

In *love*, through *language*, and finally in *masochism*, consciousness tries to absorb the other's liberty without destroying it. The other, in a sense, *possesses* my being as I shall never possess it. He gives me form, color, concreteness; and he does so freely, simply by seeing me as I am. This concrete existence, which the other confers on me, is the indication of what I should like to ground in liberty so as to be my own foundation. If I project the realization of unity with the other, this does not mean that I want him to lose his alterity, or "otherness," for if he ceased being the other he would cease being free. I want the other's liberty to become *my own possibility*. I want to assimilate the other as a free consciousness, i.e., as a subject, not as an object, i.e., as a transcended-transcendence. In order to preserve the other's subjectivity, I must first of all remain an object for him. I preciously preserve this image of myself which he has built up, in order to use it as an instrument by which I shall be able to reach his consciousness and his liberty.

In love, for instance, I want to remain the object of another's consciousness, but, as such, I want to be a limiting, or fascinating, object. Moreover the other must freely accept this limitation through constantly renewed allegiance.

Thus, in love, I want to remain an object for the other, but at the same time I want to be a limiting object, an object which the other will accept, not once for all, but again and again, as limiting his transcendence. The lover wants to be "the whole world" for the loved one. Neither the determinism of passion nor the detached attitude of elective affinity can satisfy the lover. He wants to be the occasion, not the cause of a passion. He would like to be, and to have been always, the object which the other was waiting to meet and to accept as the constant limit of any form of transcendence. He expects the loved one to *become* that self-limitation freely and constantly. But, at the same time, he wants the other to retain alterity, i.e., the negation by which the other refuses to be him. If the lover could succeed in his design, he would become, in his factual existence, the supreme value, the absolute frame of reference, his organization of the tool-things of the world would become that of the other: he would give the loved one the "stars above" together with his love; he would be a totality without losing objective concreteness. To become a limiting object, the lover has, of course, to appear as a plenum of being, to represent as much of the world as possible to the loved one, in depth, in width, in power, so that the loved one may the more easily realize the non-being of consciousness. This latter experience has already been described as fascination. Seduction aims at arousing fascination. There is no love without some form of seduction.

The use of language also implies some sort of initial self-objectification since it means adoption of the other's viewpoint concerning ourselves, even though we may aim ultimately at changing that viewpoint.

Language obviously plays an important part in love; the use we make of language is not essentially different from seduction:

> . . . it is originally the test that a being-for-itself can make of its being-for-others, and ultimately going beyond that test and using it for possibilities which are my possibilities, i.e., for possibilities of my being this and that for the other.[63]

88

To use language is to refer to my world as if it were the other's world, and to refer to myself as if I figured in that world objectively, as the others see me, in order to benefit from the contact I have established with others by changing their views to my advantage. In that respect, Shakespeare's Mark Antony is a seducer, and his speech to the Romans exemplifies the general philosophy of language. Sartre does not restrict this interpretation to the articulate word. Any form of expression has the same end. Language is not always a form of seduction, but it is always an appeal to the other's subjectivity and liberty since the other's consciousness alone can objectify my word. As an appeal to a transcendence, the use of words and signs is like the use of sacred objects which will have, at a distance, certain indefinite magical effects if I can obtain the other's freely given collaboration.

If, however, the other decides to recognize me as a free consciousness, it will be with the same purpose. He, in his turn, will try to receive recognition from my consciousness by turning into a limiting, or fascinating object. As an object, he can no longer see me objectively.

Fascination does not necessarily create love. An orator or an acrobat may fascinate one, but the general background against which they appear is only temporarily forgotten and cannot be assimilated to them. Fascination can produce love only with the loved one's consent, and that consent is given only when the loved one in his turn projects himself to be loved, i.e., to sink into objectivity before the other's subjectivity, thereby surrendering his own subjectivity. Love ends in frustration as the lovers face each other trying to be the limiting object of the other's consciousness. They had failed to realize that to love is to want to be loved, i.e., to be the *object* of the other's love. Each one remains isolated in his subjectivity, as the objectivity of one destroys the objectivity of the other. Love can only subsist as a play of reflections, each consciousness in turn reflecting the other as object, "under the ideal sign of the 'love' value, i.e., of a fusion of consciousnesses in which each one would retain its otherness to found the other." [64] To the extent that this situation implies recognition of each other's subjectivity, it may constitute a gain for both, but not the gain sought. Besides, the situation is quite unstable, as each one may suddenly use this recognition of his subjectivity to treat the other as a non-limiting object, as a tool. Moreover, it suffices that the lovers be seen together by a third person for each one to feel not only his own objectivity, but the objectivity of the other as well. This is the true reason why lovers seek solitude, and is the sense of the "deserted island" theme.

Since the subjectivity of one is exclusive of the objectivity of the other, the attempt to gain recognition as a free consciousness from another's consciousness is doomed to failure. In despair, one may decide to remain an object for the other. This is masochism.

The attempt to find, through love, the foundation of our objectivity in the subjectivity of the other by becoming a limiting object (the whole world) for that subjectivity, is doomed to failure. Realization of this fact may motivate the attempt to lose one's subjectivity altogether in the other's subjectivity, without hope of retrieving it, by becoming for the other a non-limiting object, a mere tool. This is known as masochism. Shame is the sign of one's success in this enterprise. What I am trying to do is no longer to capture a subjectivity by making of myself a fascinating object, but to allow myself to become fascinated by my own objectivity, such as it will appear to me reflected in the other's consciousness: insofar as the liberty which has absorbed my own has become the foundation of my objectivity, my being (in-itself) will be grounded in liberty and justified. This project is also doomed to failure. I cannot become fascinated by my own objectivity as reflected by the other's consciousness because I am not the other, and cannot know what sort of an object I am *for him*. I can simply guess, from outside, through the interpretation of various signs. Furthermore, in this attempt to surrender my liberty, I am using it, inasmuch as I am treating the other as a tool, i.e., as an object, which practice affirms my own subjectivity. All I can do is to experience shame, i.e., the sense of my objectivity for others. Masochism, like sadism, is assumption of guilt. I am guilty by the mere fact that I am an object for the other, and I am also guilty for having given occasion to the other for making me an object.

But one may also decide to retain one's subjectivity by forcing the other to recognize his objectivity freely; and this is sadism. Desire, hatred, and even indifference are related to this second attitude.

The second attitude toward the other is exemplified in *indifference, desire, hatred, sadism.* This attitude, in any one of these forms, may be brought about by the failure of the first attitude. Failing to capture a subjectivity through my objectivity, I may, in desperation, boldly affirm my own subjectivity and try to force the other to recognize it, which I do, first of all, by looking at him and facing his look. But you cannot face a look, at least you cannot look at a *look,* or, if you do, you only see *eyes.* So long as I succeed in being a subject for him, he apprehends himself as an object in my world, and, as such, is not in a condition freely to recognize my liberty, although he may feel its effects. The subsequent attempts I may make to force that recognition are doomed. It may be also that facing the glance of others is my original reaction to his existence, and that I chose from the first contact with him to build up my subjectivity on the collapse of the other's.

The indifferent man treats others as objects and uses them. In order to use them, he has to foresee their reactions objectively, and to use psychology. This attitude gives rise to insecurity and frustration.

This attitude is called by Sartre: *indifference to others.* The indifferent man defines people by their functions or by the use he can make of them. A whole system of psychology has been built up on the art of using people by foreseeing the reaction of the average human being, transcending his transcendence, making him an object and a tool. Such an attitude is frustrating in more ways than one. It is a kind of voluntary solipsism and blindness entailing the discomfort of losing the objectivity which alone the other can confer; it summons a sense of danger due to the fact that the other may always refuse to conform to one's calculations; it gives rise to the uneasiness which accompanies bad faith (and it is bad faith to "ignore" people whose transcendence you implicitly recognize in order to transcend it), and, finally, the few "brief and terrifying flashes," [65] signalling revelation of what the other really is, illuminate even he who has adopted indifference as a way of life.

Sexual desire is also related to sadism: it is an attempt to incarnate the consciousness of the other (to make him body-conscious) through the incarnation of our own consciousness.

Sexual desire is related to this attitude as my original attempt to get hold of the other's free subjectivity through his objectivity for me. Sexual desire and its opposite, the horror of sex, are fundamental structures of the being-for-others. Man is not sexual because he has a sex; it is the other way around. Sexuality may precede or follow (as in children and old people) its physical manifestations, and desire may not coincide with them. Let us note that desire does not aim at the end of desire, except on second thought; nor does it, except as a result of experience or hearsay, aim at the fulfilment of an act and at the pleasure derived from the fulfilment. Sexual desire is the desire for a transcendent object, but that object is a form *in a situation*. A part of the other's body arouses desire insofar as it refers to the totality of the body. The latter, in turn, refers to an attitude and to a situation in the world, an autonomous frame of reference of the world, and to the world itself. Thus, sexual desire conforms exactly to our perception of the other's body in the world. The part of my being which experiences desire is obviously my consciousness, since desire can be *only* as consciousness of desire. It is one with consciousness, but the relations that desire may entertain with its object are varied, as are the levels on which desire is experienced. Sexual desire is characterized by its "troubled" nature. "Troubled" water has all the fluidity of water, but its translucency is darkened by the presence of an invisible foreign body. In the same way, sexual desire differs by its opacity from other physiological desires, which allow consciousness to retain its lucidity. Sexual desire involves a certain complicity of consciousness with the body, a certain submission to the facticity of existence which consciousness ordinarily negates as extraneous to itself. Sexual desire is said to "seize" and to "submerge" you. One could hardly use such expressions in regard to thirst or hunger. Sexual desire is consequent to desire. It has some resemblance to sleep. In sexual desire the human look dulls, gestures are slowed down as in heavy somnolence. A sudden awakening of consciousness may make sexual desire clear and bright, as are such wants as hunger and thirst; in that case, sexual desire is viewed in itself by consciousness on the reflective plane, and is merely felt as a heavy head and a beating heart. These indications reveal sexual desire as a willingness on the part of consciousness to let itself be fascinated by the pure facticity of the body as such, and to identify itself with the body—not as expressing transcendence toward some realization, but as expressing merely the necessity of being here and now within a situation, i.e., contingent. Desire attempts to divest the other of his transcendence and to make him exist as pure flesh. It is an attempt to incarnate the consciousness of the other. To accomplish this, the other's consciousness must be compelled to reflect a being who is already incarnated: I try to make myself flesh in order to bring about the incarnation of the other. This is the only possible explanation for the practice of caresses. The caress, this ceremonial of incarnation, reveals the pure contingence of the flesh by isolating it from its transcendent possibilities; and since the person who caresses must incarnate himself in order to bring about communion in the flesh, possession is *"a double reciprocal incarnation."* [66] The

94

ultimate motive of desire is not, of course, possession of the other's body as such, but possession of a consciousness, which it represents, "possessed" by its facticity, or contingency. That is to say, through the other's contingency I want to reach his transcendence toward the world, and, in order to reach it, must temporarily give up mine. Thus, young Proust seeing Albertine play on the beach desires the whole perspective of the beach in the person of Albertine. The ideal of desire is to possess the other as transcendence and as contingency at once, and of course desire must fall. Pleasure finds its limit in the very consciousness of pleasure. It tends to become objectified (to become pleasure in itself) under the look or through the consciousness of the other. Either I become a passive object, or else, more likely, my consciousness resumes its full lucidity and I am frustrated by the fact that the other's body has become, within my hands, a mere instrument to capture a consciousness. I no longer am the free and empty reflection of a facticity which is not mine. I am frustrated without knowing why, because I cannot conceive the other's transcendence, which was the sense of my quest. Yet I may persist in that unavailing quest, and this situation is the origin of *sadism*.

Sadism also tries to incarnate the other's consciousness, to make him, with the use of tools, conscious of his body through pain and to oblige him freely to recognize his own objectivity. This attempt leads to frustration since the other as object loses his subjectivity. It may even happen that the sadist becomes the living consciousness of the other's suffering.

In sadism, consciousness is still seeking incarnation but merely through the other. It wants to enjoy the incarnation

95

of the other's consciousness in the lucidity of its own non-incarnation. It wants the other's consciousness to be entirely absorbed and fascinated by body-consciousness through pain. And that pain must be produced by instruments, even were the sadist to inflict pain through the use of his own body. The type of incarnation he wants to realize is the *obscene*. In opposition to the graceful, which reveals a transcendence related to a past situation yet perfectly adapted to its end, the obscene is disgraceful in that it reveals a freedom ill-adapted to a situation, allowing us to glimpse the other's contingency. The obscene does away with any relation of the body to the situation; it reveals the pure contingency of the flesh and its passive obedience to the law of gravitation. In the last analysis, however, what the sadist wants is the other's liberty. He does not want to destroy that liberty; he wants to appropriate it: he is waiting for the moment when the other will decide to identify himself with his tortured flesh, to yield, confess, implore. A confession made under duress is still a free confession since the victim alone decides when pain becomes unendurable. The sadist enjoys the spectacle of a struggling liberty which he knows will, sooner or later, have to admit defeat. Sadism contains the principle of its failure. As the sadist is about to reach his aim, i.e., when the victim's liberty capitulates, he faces a mere flesh object which, since his aim is to capture a liberty, he can no longer utilize. The only flesh he can incarnate is his own. Moreover, the liberty he wanted to capture was the victim's transcendent liberty, and that liberty remains in principle out of reach. The more he treats the other as an object, the more that liberty escapes him. It is a transcended-transcendence. A single look of the victim may reaffirm that transcendent liberty and the tormentor will see himself in that look as a psychic automaton, a thing among other things *in* the victim's world.

These basic attitudes do not reveal a mysterious "libido." They are various ways of facing the fact of our being-for-others. The fact that consciousness is an absolute center of reference, that we cannot face the other without becoming an object in his world for his consciousness, or else look at him as at an object within the world of our consciousness, is the fundamental basis of the sense of guilt.

These basic forms of sexual behavior are not due to a certain "libido" which creeps everywhere. They result from general attitudes which are "the fundamental projects by which the for-itself *realizes* its being-for-others and attempts to transcend that factual situation." [67] We are tossed back and forth between the other as subject and the other as object, without ever being able to apprehend him as both. Therefore, "we can never place ourselves concretely on a plane of equality, i.e., on the plane where recognition of the Other's liberty would entail recognition by the Other of our liberty." [68] Even if, as in Kantian ethics, I make the liberty of others my ultimate end, I transcend that liberty by the very fact that I have made it my aim. If I adopt the democratic definition of my liberty as a liberty which ends where the other's begins (any other, therefore, necessarily viewing my liberty as a limit to his), I make myself the limit of the other's liberty, and, if tolerance is my ideal, the other is forced to live in a tolerant world. In education, whether I adopt liberal values or not, I am still imposing a code of values on the child, and it may happen that, by imposing upon him absolute values which he has not chosen, I may develop his sense of liberty better than by letting him do what he pleases. Moreover, even in the realization of a liberal ideal, I may be in a position such as to oblige me to use other human beings, or even whole generations, as means to an end; this happens when a responsible leader decides whether or not to go into a war for the sake of liberty. No one governs innocently. Whatever I do, I have to do it in a world where the other also exists, and where I seem to be in excess (*de trop*).

> It is from that peculiar situation that the notion of culpability and sin seems to draw its origin. It is facing the other that I feel *guilty*. Guilty first when under his look I experience my alienation and my nudity as a fall which I must assume; this is the meaning of the famous: "They knew that they were nude" of the Scripture. Guilty moreover, when in my turn, I look at the other, because, by the very fact of my affirming my self, I constitute him an object and an instrument, and bring about for him the alienation which he will have to assume. Thus, the original sin is my surging into a world where there is the other, and, whatever my ulterior relations with the other may be, they will be variations on the original theme of my culpability.[69]

All I can do, then, is give the other occasions to manifest his liberty. It may happen that, in the light of my experience or private history, I may become resigned to give up any form of being-for-others, and simply aim at their destruction. This attitude is known as *hatred*. Hatred wants to do away with the other as transcendence, and, to do so, it must first recognize his transcendence. This is why any manifestation of liberty may arouse hatred, even a generous act. Hatred is a fundamental attitude aiming at the others in general through the other in particular, which explains why it is held in general disrepute. Hatred also fails to reach its aim; as I suppress the other, I become the living memory of his existence, his reflection, his consciousness. From then on, he is part of me, a part which I can neither obliterate nor modify.

Being with *others is distinct from being for others.*

The preceding descriptions do not account for *being with others,* i.e., the feeling of harmony we may experience at belonging to a community. This mode of being, referred to by Heidegger as the *"Mitsein"* (being together), is expressed by the pronouns "we" and "us." The subject form "we," however, as we shall see later, refers to a common action which is expressed by the verb. It expresses *doing-with* rather than *being-with.* As an audience, for instance, we *are* together only insofar as we *react* together to the play. The original sense of *being* together is revealed to *us,* as objects.

This mode of being—Heidegger's Mitsein—*basically corresponds to the sense of being objectified along* with *others. Only in self-defense does a group assume common subjectivity which in the eyes of the dictator constitutes a form of mass masochism. Reference to the whole of humanity does not eliminate the notion of the other carried to its conceptual limit: God.*

Us refers to the experience of human beings who are objectified together. This experience may be illustrated by the now familiar experience of the human looked at by one person. If I am being looked at by two persons, I still view the others as subjects, but I tend to depersonalize that subjectivity and to feel that someone is looking at me. If the third person looks at the second person, who is looking at me, the third transcendence transcends the transcendence which transcends mine, thereby contributing to disarm it. I may then ally myself with the third party and look at the second, who will become our common object, or I may look at the third, who is looking at the second, who is looking at me; or else I may look at both the second and the third, disarm the look of the third party and make them both objects for me. In this case, I may experience, through the second, the look of the third party which is fixed upon him; he still appears as an object, but not as an object *for me*. He may resent the fact that I look at him while he is being looked at. The second and the third parties may then look at me again to affirm in common their subjectivity. It is, in any case, the presence of the third party as subject which determines the consciousness of the "us." "Us" refers to a common objectification, to a sentiment of solidarity within that objectification. It expresses a factual situation which has to be assumed and which corresponds to the vanishing of the "we": "We were engaged in a conflict when he came upon us." It is, of course, a humiliating experience, one which is particularly felt by any group conscious of being used by somebody or by another group. And since, to be felt, consciousness of the other requires neither the experience of his look, nor of his actual presence, some plurality of individuals is always bound to feel that it is being used, or objectified, by some other group or by the whole of humanity. Hence class or nation consciousness. Class consciousness is due neither to a feeling of common misery nor to oppression. It is the feeling of existing for and through the liberty of the other. "Thus the oppressed class finds its class unity in the cognizance which the oppressing class takes of it, and the appearance in the oppressed of class-consciousness corresponds to the assumption, in shame, of an 'us.' " [70] The oppressed class will react by the project of transforming the "us" into a "we" through the affirmation of its subjectivity and of its

100

transcendence. It will try, in self-defense, to objectify the ruling class, simply by treating it as a class: "They." Unless, however, it decides on the opposite attitude which is to prefer forgetting its subjectivity in the fascination exercised by the look, the voice, and the person of some dictator. In this case, and, we presume, in some other cases, the "we" may express an assumed objectivity: "You fascinate *us; we* worship you, O Master!" In all such cases, a section of humanity could refer to itself as "us" (or as a "we" objectified). When we refer to the whole of humanity in this manner, we still retain the notion of the other carried to its conceptual limit, i.e., the notion of God.

We do experience a sort of collective subjectivity when we use signs, instructions and fabricated objects to reach ends which we share with others. But signs, instructions, etc., are meant for an interchangeable and inexistent human being. It is what Heidegger calls the "unauthentic Mitsein." *The team spirit corresponds to a more authentic sense of transcendence toward a common aim; in this case, however,* being with others *can be reduced to* doing with others.

The world, however, and the presence of manufactured objects within the world, proclaim that we also belong to a community of subjects. These artifacts have been wrought for undifferentiated and absent transcendent subjects; the tin can was prepared so that someone might open it, and the opening of a tin can is a manifestation of the way in which we transcend inert matter to make it instrumental to our ends. As I open the tin can, I am a transcendent "someone." The sort of transcendence I experience is depersonalized. It was foreseen by the manufacturer who formulated the instructions on the can. In the same way, when I follow the signs to find my way in the subway, I forget the individual purpose of my trip; I am one of the other travellers; I am, as far as the instructions given by the signs concern me, an interchangeable human being of the type Heidegger refers to as "one," "they," "people." This is a form of *Mitsein*. If, on the other hand, I am proceeding with others toward a common aim, as, for instance, in an attack, or am simply working with them toward the realization of a common enterprise, I experience a different sort of collective feeling. I am then engaged in a project which I have made mine, a project which is present to me in the very rhythm of common action with its future and its past. It would seem that such a form of transcendence is at once collective and subjective. Let us not, however, forget that, in such a case, I experience the transcendence of others *alongside* of my own, as a transcendence which has the same object as mine. It is felt neither objectively nor quite subjectively. It is felt rather as a *common rhythm* of action. It is properly speaking, the team-spirit; not a real *Mitsein,* but a *Mitmachen;* not a *being-together,* but a *doing-together:*

And, no doubt, this experience may be sought as the symbol of an absolute and metaphysical unity of all transcendences; it seems, indeed, that it suppresses the original conflict of transcendences by making them converge toward the world; in this sense, the ideal *we* (*nous-sujet*) would be the *we* of a humanity which would be making itself master of the world. But the experience of the *we* remains on the ground of individual psychology and remains a simple symbol of the desirable unity of transcendences; it is in no way, indeed, a lateral and real apprehension of subjectivities as such by a single subjectivity; the subjectivities remain out of reach and radically separated.[71]

102

We should, however, not pass too lightly over this important concession from Sartre. It would seem, according to this passage, that the world might, on the plane of action, if not on that of pure being, serve as a mediator between otherwise irreconcilable subjectivities: "I learn that I am a part of a *we* through the world." [72] It is true that such an experience does not imply that others experience it with me. As to the fact that I am surrounded by the objects of man's industry, it does not constitute my primordial revelation of the existence of others; that revelation, as we have seen, comes to me from different sources. It merely refers to my undifferentiated transcendence. The existence of the *we* constitutes a provisional appeasement in the midst of conflict, not a definite solution of the conflict. The conflict of transcendence is the original state of being for others. This is why there is no class-consciousness among the privileged. As subjects, they consider themselves mere individuals. The "bourgeois" does not recognize himself as such, and, in fact, defines himself as an individual consciousness which denies the existence of classes; to him they seem the artificial creation of a few leaders. It is only when he is the object of his employees' resentment that he discovers kinship with others of the same social standing, and is tempted to say: "We, the employers." In our existence for others we discover ourselves primarily as subjects. The essence of the rapports between consciousnesses is conflict, not *Mitsein*.

V *Being-In-Itself-For-Itself*

1. Doing and being: liberty.

Having and doing *are existential categories which can be explained in terms of* being: *this is the* ontological reduction.

We just saw that what applies to being may not always be true on the plane of doing. The existential categories of doing and having can, in the last analysis, be explained in terms of being, and this analysis Sartre calls *ontological reduction.* But this reduction can be made only under the sign of the ideal value of being-in-itself-for-itself, which has been mentioned so far only incidentally, although it is implied in many passages. We shall therefore place the description of doing and having under that ideal sign, although Sartre treats it separately.

Action is intentional, whether we choose to act emotionally or deliberately. It manifests the liberty of the for-itself and its non-being. The for-itself is not, but has to make itself.

The first condition of action is liberty. Any action is intentional, although its results may extend beyond the intention. Blowing up a powder-house by absent-mindedly throwing away a burning cigarette is not acting. Any intention involves a double negating process. On the one hand, an ideal and non-existing situation must be posited as a present non-being, and on the other the actual situation must be considered as a non-being in relation to the ideal situation. No purely factual state of affairs can by itself motivate an action. Historians have often noticed that revolutions spring out of new hopes, not out of present miseries. It is only when a hope is born that present conditions, transcended toward that hope, appear as intolerable. There must be rupture with the present; consciousness must cancel it by dissociating itself from it. In this sense, Hegel correctly stated that "mind is the negative." Motivation, the act, and the end surge together as the expression of freedom. The surge of liberty is an existential phenomenon which remains undefinable if I persist in considering liberty as an essence. I cannot describe liberty in general, the liberty of the other, or of all men; I can only describe my liberty. Its concrete experience is given to my consciousness in the negating process. It is through this negating process that the for-itself escapes from its being as from its essence:

> it is through it that . . . (the for-itself) is at least that which escapes that very denomination, that which is already beyond the name which one gives it, the property which one recognizes in it. To say that the for-itself has to be what it is, to say that it is what it is not while not being

what it is, to say that in its existence precedes and conditions essence, or inversely, following Hegel's formula, that for it *"Wesen ist was gewesen ist,"* is to say one and the same thing, i.e., that man is free. From the very fact, indeed, that I am conscious of the motives which solicit my action, these motives are already transcendent objects for my consciousness, they are outside; in vain shall I seek to cling to them: I escape from them through my very existence. I am condemned to exist forever beyond my essence, beyond the affective and rational motives of my act: I am condemned to be free.[73]

Determinism is the attempt to establish within us an unbroken continuity of being-in-itself. Psychologically, it comes back to trying to consider motives as *things* having a permanent character, while, in reality, I confer them permanence, or refuse to do so, from day to day. Or else the future ends of my action may be offered as an explanation for my action, but they will be taken as having been met by chance, or as I came into the world: they came to me from God, nature, "my" nature, society. At any rate, I have not elected them freely. Such explanations collapse before the experience of anguish wherein I find at once the non-being and the freedom of the for-itself. The non-being in the heart of man compels human reality to *make itself* instead of *being*. A rather common conception assimilates liberty with the will. But will is merely a reflective attitude assumed in relation to certain ends which liberty, and not the will, has chosen. Voluntary deliberation is always faked anyway, says Sartre. In deliberating pros and cons, I am trying to treat motives as things that may be weighed and possess permanent values. It is simply a manner of proceeding, since I confer them these values; and this manner of proceeding constitutes an attempt at self-recuperation, i.e., the realization of my being-in-itself-and-for-itself: "I did what I wanted to do." Often, as we all know, deliberation produces opposite results, and our ends appear to us vitiated by thought. Passion may pursue the same ends in a different way. There are, as La Rochefoucauld once said, certain situations from which it takes a certain madness to escape. Before the same danger, one may choose to obey the passion of fear or decide to resist, without rejecting his allegiance to the value of self-preservation. In fear, I seek symbolic fulfilment by not facing the situation, by distancing myself from the world together with my consciousness of it; in rational behavior, I try to modify it through knowledge. But in both cases, I have rejected it in the light of the same value. This does not mean our behavior is *determined* by values; it means that we not only choose our values, but also the very manner in which we choose to be free.

Our particular, or secondary, projects are related to a fundamental individual project.

Liberty is, however, related to an original project concerning our being. It is not an irrational and purely contingent whim. In a military march, one soldier will enjoy the very feeling of fatigue. Through fatigue, he experiences at once the factual existence of his body, the action of the world (the roads, the hills to be climbed) on his body, and the transcendent movement of his march onwards. He is at once for-himself, in the sentiment of his progression toward an aim, and in-himself, through the feeling of bodily fatigue which permeates his consciousness. He is at least aiming at this equilibrium which has a symbolic value for him. His behavior may refer to an attitude elected earlier in his life: the athletic attitude; this in turn may refer to an earlier attitude leading to a fundamental project concerning the relations of the for-itself to the in-itself, beyond which there is no possible regress. Another man will drop on the side of the road because, to him, the feeling of fatigue is intolerable. This again may refer to an attitude assumed at a younger age. He is "soft" because he has chosen to experience the facticity of his body on the plane of "abandonment," or indulgence. This attitude also refers to a fundamental project concerning the relation of the for-itself to the in-itself. Sartre's view is here confirmed by the fact that a physical handicap is often an inducement and a challenge to athletic performance.

Our individual projects can be determined by existential psychoanalysis. Existential psychoanalysis differs from Freudian psychoanalysis in that it seeks the motivation of our actions in a project freely adopted at an early age, rather than in some determining circumstance encountered at that early age.

This original project may be determined through existential psychoanalysis. Like Freud, Sartre explains our actions through a *Weltanschauung,* rather than through a cause and effect relationship which relates one moment of our life to the next on the plane of psychic determinism: I knocked him down because I felt insulted. Freud, however, re-establishes a sort of vertical determinism through his "kobold in the cellar," the subconscious libido, and the determination of complexes by the libido at an early age. There is no future dimension for Freudian psychoanalysis; it works from the present to the past through an objective witness. Sartre rejects Freudian theory, but he accepts the method of the objective witness provided it be used in the opposite direction. I cannot *know* what my original project is because I *am* that project; but another person could find out what this project is through my reactions to situations, things, and the qualities of things. The way I succumb to fatigue is not due to some distant complex contracted in the past, not even an Adlerian complex of inferiority; or, rather, the complex of inferiority itself is a project of my for-itself-in-the-world-for-the-other. It is still a transcendence and must be explained in the light of the end it represents. It is the solution I have adopted in regard to the existence of the other, that insurmountable scandal. Psychoanalysis, then, should consider the immediate possibility which is the end of the action, and the possibilities which it leads to until the ultimate possibility, which will define my manner of being, is reached. Through regressive analysis, it should return to the action in question to grasp its "integration within the total form." To understand what Sartre means by "the total form," we must go back to his definition of the world-as-background. We do not discover the world as we pass within the world from one object to the next. On the contrary, the world is at first perceived by consciousness as totality. On the background of that totality, which is the sum total of its possibilities, consciousness detaches objects one by one. As I come from the world to a particular "this," I come to a singled-out possibility of mine, and, just as I cannot grasp a "this" except on world-background, I cannot project myself beyond the "this" toward such or such a possibility except on the background of my ultimate and total possibility. Thus, the world sends me back an image of myself which I can only decipher through action, but which someone else may decipher objectively as the outline of a solution to the problem of being. It is, however, to be deciphered not only on the plane of *doing,* but on the plane of *having* as well, through interpretation of the symbolic appropriation of things and of the qualities of things.

109

Not only do I choose a fundamental project concerning my existence, but I also choose among the various possibilities which are offered me to live according to that project.

The choice I can make of a certain possibility is part of my fundamental project, but some possibilities are directly related to it and some are indifferent. As in the Gestalt theory, the choice of a "form" on a "background" may involve variations in the secondary structure of that form. The fact that, being tired of walking, I decide to sit a while on the side of the road, rather than walk another mile and stop at the inn, entails no difference in relation to my project, which is to reach the next town. These "indifferent" possibilities merely constitute new manifestations and enrichments of our freedom. Alone, the subject can interpret the connections he establishes between primary and secondary ends; he is even free to choose actions which are contrary to his ultimate ends, but this only happens on the reflective plane. Immediate consciousness can never be deceived about its ends. If my project is to go through life as inferior, my "complex of inferiority" may express itself through stammering; I may decide on a purely reflective plane to rid myself of that defect by technical means and succeed in doing so. But my feeling of inferiority will only be displaced to affirm itself in other ways. I may choose to be inferior by selecting a field of action in which I cannot succeed. I may decide, still on the reflective plane, to be a great artist and struggle for recognition. This will not be, as Adler thinks, a subconscious attempt of my frustrated will-to-power to compensate for my sense of inferiority; it will be the means I have chosen to maintain in myself the sense of inferiority. If I do not recognize the fact, it is because my reflection interposes between my spontaneous consciousness and my ultimate

110

end the concepts of "art," "worship of beauty," and "glory." There is no subconscious for Sartre, but there is a spontaneous consciousness of one's ultimate end which may not know itself, and the part played by inhibition in the Viennese school may, in Sartre, be played by the bad faith inherent to reflection in its "impure" form.

My liberty even goes as far as to allow me to change my fundamental project anytime. This can happen only in the light of a new project which involves a breaking away from my past and a full realization of my present situation.

This does not mean that I have to live my fundamental project to the end. But in order to change it, I must first see it objectively in its totality. The liberating instant which will objectify this life-project and make it a past may arise suddenly in the light of a new project, heralded by anguish and by the fear of becoming other than I am. Such conversions, Sartre notes, have not been studied by philosophers but have often inspired men of letters. They give us "the clearest and most stirring image of our liberty." [74] Anyone can recall having come across descriptions of such conversions in the works of Huxley or of Sartre himself. The liberating instant is at once a beginning and an end within the unity of a single act. It belongs to the future as a beginning, and is related to the past as an end. A converted atheist is not merely a Christian; he is a Christian who *negates* his *past* atheism.

It is our liberty which brings the situation to light.

To sum up that part of the foregoing which concerns action: Man finds his being only in the act. The existence of

111

the act implies its autonomy. To differ from pure movement, the act must be defined by an intention. The intention reveals itself through the world and the world is defined by the intention. The surge of an intention means rupture with the datum, or situation, but it also brings the situation to light. Being negation of its identity with the datum, consciousness is not conditioned by it. The datum is, however, its foundation and there could be no liberty without it. My fundamental project is my being; it can be modified by liberty alone in the light of a new project, and it has to be objectified in its totality to be transcended.

The situation is not an obstacle to liberty; or rather it is liberty itself which defines it as an obstacle in the light of a particular project. Liberty is inconceivable outside of a situation, and there is no situation outside of liberty. My body, my position in the world, and my past are all part of my situation.

The situation is the facticity of liberty. The argument of common sense is that we cannot change the situation in which we were born. I am born in a certain class, citizen of a certain nation, with a certain heredity. The slightest modification of these data takes years and I have first to conform to circumstances to change them. It would seem that I am what circumstances make me, and that I cannot control them. These arguments have never succeeded in destroying our intimate sense of liberty, nor in convincing the partisans of liberty. The adversity of things appears only in regard to the end pursued. A mountain appears as something to be climbed to the Alpinist; to the traveller, it appears as an obstacle to be avoided. Moreover, to be free does not mean "obtaining what one wishes" but "to determine oneself to wish." Liberty is autonomy of choice. A captive is not free to leave his prison, but he is free to attempt an escape. Obstacles are the very proof of liberty; only liberty meets obstacles. Liberty exists only in relation to time, space, and circumstances. The facts that I *have* to be free (the *facticity* of liberty), am the particular being that I have to be (the *contingency* of liberty), and the *datum* (the *situation* within which I find myself), are one and the same thing; and that situation appears only in the light of a liberty which refuses to identify itself with it and faces a still non-existing end. This datum is, of course, the being-in-itself negated by the for-itself, the body being its center of reference, the past its essence. Liberty lights the world in a philosophical sense since, in order to project itself toward an end, it has to establish a system of relationships between the things of the world, as background for the being it has to attain. It is impossible to distinguish within a given situation what belongs to the contingency of the in-itself and what belongs to liberty. For instance, the mountain will appear to me impossible to climb only in the light of projecting to climb it, which intention relates to the fundamental project constituting my way of being in the world. Whether the nature of the rock is such as to allow me to climb the mountain is a different matter, but only within a situation created by a would-be climber could there be resistance to climbing. For a mere tourist in quest of aesthetic delight, the rock appears neither easy nor difficult to climb, but as having such a shape or color. Moreover, my evaluation of the resistance to be encountered in the execution of a project varies according to the importance I attribute to its realization. The paradox of liberty is then that there is no liberty outside of a situation and no situation outside of liberty; not only my body but the place I occupy in the world, my past and my position among others are all part of my situation.

The fact that I live in a certain locality constitutes a situation for me only inasmuch as I have projected to live elsewhere, or inasmuch as I have adopted a certain manner of being consisting in wishing to be where I am not.

The place I occupy in the world, in a certain country, at a certain distance from certain objects, refers to my original contingency. Even if I came there freely, I had to arrive from another place, and, in retracing my steps, I find myself in the place where I was quite unconditionally; a pure contingency. At the same time, it is because I am free that I can say that I occupy a certain place at a certain distance from other places. "You are going quite far," said someone to an internationalist about to leave for Argentina. "Far from what?" asked the internationalist who had ceased to consider France his home. To conceive myself as occupying a certain place, I have, in a sense, to dissociate myself from that place, to transcend it toward certain other places which permit me to locate my own: I am so many hours away from Peter by train and have to drive so many hours to see Anny. My ends create the situation; they are felt in the symbolic significance I give to the locations. Having climbed the mountain, I am "on top of the world," at sea I am "away from it all." Places have existential meanings for me which recall the manner of being I have chosen for myself through life. The restrictions imposed upon my liberty by my location in space are proofs of my liberty; it is because I want to live in New York that I feel so conscious of being located in Podunk. If my project is insincere, it is just a way of perpetually negating my existence in Podunk.

My past constitutes a situation for me merely in relation to some project concerning the future.

Our past does not determine our future, nor does it constitute our present. But neither can it be ignored by liberty, for liberty exists only in relation to its past and in function of its past. I have to recognize my past, were it only to revolt against it, since it is my concrete being-in-itself. The present is presence to a past, and my past follows me into the present: *Wesen ist was gewesen ist.* The position I chose, the house I built, the suit I bought are part of me, the being whom I *have to* be. I cannot think of myself without thinking of my past since I am that past; but if I can think the past and bring it into being, that is because I survey it in the light of the future. My transcendence would have no meaning if I did not have a past to transcend. Yet, if it is true that consciousness is always consciousness of something, it is also true that whatever is in consciousness is there as being questioned, which means that nothing appears to consciousness without being chosen. No element of my past appears to my consciousness without bearing some relation to my future projects. The meaning I confer on past incidents varies according to the nature of these projects. Outside of that constant evaluation, my past, no doubt, is made up of raw data, constituting the matter of Bergson's "pure memory," and I can explore that past, as did Proust; but such exploration involves a project of its kind.

As our fundamental project in life is confirmed or altered, the meaning of our past actions changes accordingly.

115

TO BE AND NOT TO BE

The meaning of my past actions depends on my present project, which is part of my life-project. I determine that meaning not by deliberation, but by acting on my projects. The mystical crisis through which I went at the age of fifteen will acquire the meaning of a premonition if at twenty or thirty I become converted. The force of the past is conferred by my projects, i.e., by the future. Between full acceptance of the past and its complete disavowal, there are ambiguous states. I may reassume the conjugal bond daily because it is part of my life-project to be a good husband and a good father. I may just respect that bond, although my fundamental values have changed, because a settled way of life suits my present purpose. I may reject it altogether, under the impulse of a spiritual quest, like Mallory's Galahad, or of an aesthetic quest, like Gauguin, in one of those rare instants where our life-projects undergo a complete change. The past may be living, half-alive, preserved in an ambiguous way, disavowed.

This is true of the history of nations, the past events of which receive new meanings from events in the making.

This applies to the history of human societies. The participation of the United States in the first World War may have been due to certain considerations bearing on the future of that country. In the light of such considerations, it may have been found expedient to remember that America had a debt of honor to pay back to France, because such emotional motivation is useful in obtaining the adhesion of the masses. Nevertheless, the past, thus interpreted, assumed historical force with the famous "Lafayette, we are here!" Through this interpretation, a new past, so to speak, had been created, a tradition inaugurated, which the discovery of actual affinities

116

between two capitalistic democracies merely confirmed. Thus, the past is always subject to a new interpretation. Was the storming of the Bastille in 1789 a mere episode which the Convention, for reasons of publicity, decided to consecrate as a symbolic and glamorous intervention of the popular will which, strengthened and confirmed by this action, gave a new direction to the whole movement? The historian can only decide on such points in the light of his own tendencies and of those of his times: the historian is also historical. History is a continuous "reprieve."

The fact that, instead of taking our surroundings for granted, we consider them as obstacles to our liberty merely proves that we are free.

My surroundings are made up of objects which may figure in my projects as obstacles or as utensils. If they are obstacles, they simply confirm the existence of liberty, which will have to manifest itself against them. Any project of liberty is an *open* project, which has to take into account the possible adversity of things, and implies the possibility of its own modifications. This is why the obstacles we encounter in the realization of our plans so often bear a familiar look: "I could have sworn this was going to happen!" Liberty confers adversity on things and brings them to existence at the same time.

Laws, customs, prejudices, beliefs, language, techniques may seem to confer on my world, and the things of my world, meanings which I have not chosen; they are the conditions of my liberty; either I adopt them freely or I admit their factual existence in order to modify or refute them.

117

My fellowman, however, obliges me to see in the objects which surround me something more than obstacles or utensils. To be concrete, my situation in the world must be considered as related to objects which already have a signification: the poster, the street, the station, have significations which are already mine since they point to my race, my nationality, my physique, and they also point to centers of reference which are not my own, but those of the Other. Indeed my world is made significant to me in numberless ways through the existence of the other. Whatever I do, my behavior is dictated to me by signs, notices, roads, traffic lights, etc. This would seem to limit my liberty, since any of my projects will have to borrow means of execution which I have to accept as a matter of fact. To express myself, I have to obey the technique of a particular language without having had anything to do with the elaboration of that technique. Through the fact of language, it would seem that I am thrown into a system of meanings, an interpretation of the riddle of the universe which I have not chosen. The dialect I am using, the language to which this dialect belongs, define, from outside, my existence insofar as I am part of a collective group. Yet, if the truth of the dialect lies in the language to which it belongs, the truth of that language belongs to language in general, which in turn reflects even more universal structures of consciousness. To that extent, it is not true that the use of a certain dialect necessarily confers a certain view of the world. Linguists have pointed out that the word has no meaning outside of the sentence, and that even groups of words or clichés may change meaning in different paragraphs. If so, neither words, nor syntax, nor even clichés have an existence of their own before we make use of them:

The verbal unity being the significant phrase, the latter is a constructive act which may be understood only through a transcendence which goes beyond, and negates, the datum [as it projects itself] toward an end. To understand the word in the light of the sentence is *very exactly* to understand any datum from the situation, and to understand the situation in the light of the original ends. To understand a sentence of the man addressing me is indeed to understand what he *"means,"* i.e., . . . to throw myself forward, with him, toward possibilities, toward ends, and then to come back to the ensemble of organized means to understand them according to their function and their aim.[75]

Words may seem to have a life of their own, because they reflect some past trail of human thought, but they come to life again only within the phrase, which is a project, and as such can be interpreted only in the light of a project, which, in its turn, can be understood only as the negation of a given situation. Language has sometimes been understood as having its own laws, a "nature" of its own, independent of the liberty of the speaker; this is because it has been considered as *once spoken,* without any regard to the fact that while *it is being spoken,* it is borne on a human liberty. The error of linguists has been to consider language as having a kind of magic life of its own. "This is the error to be avoided in regard to language, as in regard *to any other technique."* [76] The study of techniques will never help us to discover the technician. If words can be related to each other, it is because a certain subjective unity has been projected into expression by the speaker. Alone the listener can *objectively* break down the sentence into its elements, analyse its structures and formulate its laws. What is true of language is true of other aspects of social life: government, laws, customs, prejudices, scientific notions, beliefs; they are the conditions of my liberty, and I have to

admit their factual existence in order to modify them or to
refute them.

*The liberty of others, however, does limit my own insofar as
I exist objectively in their consciousness which defines me according to race, trade, type, etc. All I can do in this respect is
to accept this limitation as an external limitation.*

The only true limit to my liberty is the liberty of others, for
only liberty can limit liberty. I can give a personal meaning to
the things, tools, and techniques I find around me, but I cannot give a meaning to that *object* which I *am* for the liberty
of the others. I cannot give it meaning, because I am *objectively* for him alone. He possesses a dimension of my being
which escapes me. To that extent, I am, for the other, something I have not chosen to be. I can neither reject this existence which is conferred on me from outside, for this would
amount to voluntary solipsism, nor conform to it as long as I
retain consciousness and freedom. All I can do is to recognize
the fact that I exist in the consciousness of others, as I recognize their liberty; to make it part of the general situation
which I have to act upon. Thus, at least, the limitation conferred on me by the notions others entertain about me will
remain external limitations; it is for the others that I am a
Jew, a worker, a Frenchman. I have to accept these limitations
conferred on me from outside by others, as they define me
according to race, nationality, and physical appearance; my
liberty will never coincide with them.

*Death alone, as the end of my possibilities, can suppress my
liberty. It is not true that death gives to life a definite meaning: it is the end of all meanings for me. If death comes from*

120

outside, it is a mere contingency; if it is voluntary, its meaning is to bring about the end of all meanings for me, and it is therefore absurd.

The only end of my possibilities is death. Attempts have been made, particularly by Heidegger, to consider death, not as a passage into non-being, but as a purely human event, the last of the series and the most meaningful: the end of *life*. Death considered thus would give its sense to existence, as its supreme achievement in the same way as the last note of the melody, rebounding, as it were, on all the preceding notes, gives its definite sense to the melody. To Sartre, death is as contingent and as absurd as birth is. One may decide to give a meaning to one's life through a glorious death of liberation, and be run over on the way to the recruiting office. Besides, one can prepare for *a particular* death, but not for one's death. Heidegger says that to die is my most individual realization, the only thing that no one can do for me, and that my whole life should be oriented toward death; but even if my death were not accidental, if I die of old age, it still is a biological fact. Death is not my possibility, but a negation of my possibilities which does not depend upon me. The meaning of my life is always an expectation; if death is the end of all expectations, how could it give a meaning to my life? No meaning can be conferred from outside. A young man with great literary ambition may die after producing his first book; if it is good, he will be considered by posterity as a one-book man, if it is bad, he will be completely forgotten. If Balzac had died young, he would be considered by posterity as one among many 19th century writers of mediocre "black" novels. The whole meaning he wanted to impart to his existence would have been lost. Death is not what gives life its meaning; on the contrary, it is what takes away from life any meaning. Suicide itself cannot be said to have meaning for me, since alone the future can confer meaning, and since suicide, being the last act of my life, rejects the future. If I "miss myself," I shall be able to confer meaning on that act, call it cowardly, stupid, or courageous; otherwise, being without a future, my suicide is also deprived of meaning and is properly absurd.

It is only for the others that my death has any meaning, and it is up to them to define that meaning. Death consecrates my being for others in itself, i.e., as an object.

It is for others that my life assumes with death a definite character. Through death, my life ceases to be a perpetual reprieve; it is achieved and completely in itself. If I am well-known its character, in funerary oration, articles, biographies, history, will be conferred on it by others; if I am not, by the family tradition and by my friends, until I sink into oblivion as a person and become lost for history in a collectivity designated as the middle-class or the proletariat of such or such an age. For to be forgotten is not to be reduced to nothing, according to Sartre; it is to lose one's personal existence and assume a collective one for posterity. Part of our existence for others consists in the position we take in regard to the dead. As I live my projects, I have to adopt an attitude toward the institutions and collectivities of the past; the Inquisition confirms me in my anti-Catholic stand, the excesses of the French Revolution in my conservative convictions. My generation, as a collectivity engaged in a certain effort, confers new meanings on certain events and personalities of history, as the America of 1917 did for Lafayette; but these transformations of the past occur, of course, only through and for the living, from outside. For the dead, "the chips are down." Death is the triumph of the Other. All in all, death is merely a certain aspect of facticity and of being-for-others, i.e., nothing but a datum.

The situation, in its universal and particular structures, is my chance to exercise my liberty.

To sum up, then, what Sartre understands by situation: I realize my position in the world only in the light of a project. The situation exists only in correlation with the use of a datum toward an end. There is no privileged situation in regard to liberty; I am just as free in one as in another. The situation contains abstract and universal structures, but it must be understood as the single face which the world turns upon us, as our unique and personal chance. As I project myself toward my ends through the world, I encounter sequences and connected series; I establish laws to utilize them and further my ends. The situation accounts for our substantial permanence; our past, our character, the judgment of others have the permanence of being in itself, which we may easily confuse with our own permanence. In particular, the character conferred on me by others has a concreteness which I may, according to my life-project, accept in fascination or reject through rebellion. I may use it to "build myself up," or I may resent it inasmuch as it makes me feel "hemmed in." Death is the consecration of the others' viewpoint.

I am responsible for the situation in its universal as well as in its particular aspect: for myself, for the others (inasmuch as I transcend their transcendence), for the world. I experience

123

this responsibility in anguish when I do not run away from it in bad faith. Although my birth and the situation in which I was born are contingent facts, I assume them by existing and adopting a fundamental attitude toward them.

Man is responsible for himself and for the world. He makes himself responsible for himself when he assumes his fundamental manner of being; he is responsible for the world, for situation is only one aspect of his liberty. I am as responsible for the war as if I had declared it myself. It is part of my situation. I cannot ignore that situation, or rather, if I do ignore it, I am merely manifesting my liberty by ignoring it, as I might by endorsing it, or treating it as a vacation. As soon as I am born, I become responsible for the world. This latter responsibility is, however, of a particular type. I am born responsible, which means that I am responsible for everything except my very responsibility, for I am not the foundation of my being. I am forsaken in the world, not as a piece of wreckage, but as a free being to whom full responsibility for this world has been committed. Whatever attitude I may choose in regard to the event of my birth, this attitude involves a project concerning my mode of being, which involves my assumption of the fact that I was born. Since any event of the world can only appear to me as an occasion or a chance, i.e., as a way to the realization of that being which is questioned within my being, and since the others, as transcended transcendences, are also occasions and chances for us to pursue that realization, the responsibility of the for-itself extends to the whole of the populated world, and this is the reason why our liberty is apprehended in anguish. Most of the time, however, we seek escape in bad faith.

124

•

2. Man's fundamental project—the individual project—existential psychoanalysis.

Liberty is not a whim. Consciousness aims at being, which means that the end of the for-itself is the in-itself, but not the contingent in-itself which is precisely what the for-itself nihilates: "Nihilation, as we saw, can be assimilated to a revolt of the in-itself which nihilates itself against its contingency." [77] The for-itself wants to acquire as *consciousness* the infinite density of the in-itself:

> the for-itself projects to be *as for-itself* a being which is what it is; it is as a being which is what it is not and which is not what it is that the for-itself projects to be what it is; it is as consciousness that it wants to have the impermeability and the infinite-density of the in-itself; it is as nihilation of the in-itself and as perpetual escape from contingence and facticity that it wants to be its own foundation. That is why the possible is projected in general as what the for-itself lacks to become in-itself-for-itself, and the fundamental value which presides over this project is precisely the in-itself-for-itself, i.e., the ideal of a consciousness which would be the foundation of its own being-in-itself through the pure consciousness which it would take of itself. It is this ideal which one may call God.[78]

We may say then that: "To be a man is to tend to be God; or, if one prefers, man is fundamentally the desire to be God." [79]

This does not mean that there is a human nature, *or an essence of man, outside of man. Man's fundamental project is merely an ideal value.*

Does not this fundamental human project confer a "nature" on man, and define his "essence" in such a way as to

125

limit his liberty? If there is only one end to all human activities, will it not become possible to tell what any man will do in any given situation? Sartre's answer to this objection is that if there is such an essence of man, it is merely an abstraction which does not at all precede and determine his existence, but merely gives the truth, or the meaning of individual liberty. It is an ideal value which cannot be realized, and, concretely, there are only individual projects which bear on what to do with one's contingency. The individual has to invent a particular manner of being; and to realize this manner of being, he has to invent his ends and build up situations out of contingent surroundings. Going from the particular to the general, we find that empirical desire is the symbolic form adopted in the fundamental and individual project which defines the person; this individual project is a form of the human project to realize being-in-itself-for-itself. But, of course, this human project exists only in the form which we can identify as *the person*.

The individual project constitutes the person, and because it is the person, the subject does not, in general, know the nature of the project. As in Freudian psychoanalysis, it would take another person to objectify the subject's fundamental project.

How can we reach this individual life-project which might give us the clue to the secondary projects, or desires, of a person? Psychology may go as far as establishing a list of empirical desires, and even point out certain relations between them. The understanding of the life-projects which diversify persons, and constitute persons, is a different matter. It could be reached only through an existential psychoanalysis. The principle of such psychoanalysis would be that every form of behavior, to the most trifling gesture, is revealing. Its method would consist in the comparison of the subject's patterns of behavior in various circumstances, and in the detection of the fundamental project which it symbolizes. Like Freud's psychoanalysis, it would seek the origin of the individual's fundamental attitude in a reaction to a certain situation encountered in an early past. It would not, however, try to detect a fixation of the libido, but the original choice. As in Freud, the analysis would have to be carried out by another person than the subject, at least in most cases. Sartre does not believe in the subconscious; but the fact that one is conscious of one's fundamental project does not mean that one knows that project. So long as we live a project which concerns our innermost mode of being, we lack the detachment required by analysis. The reflective process may furnish data to the psychoanalyst, but it does not disclose the subject's fundamental project. This project can only be objectified as a transcended-transcendence, even if the subject is trying to psychoanalyze himself. Definition of that project would account at once for the situation and for the choice. No general and universal motivation would be sought as applicable to all human behavior. Sexuality only expresses an effort at recuperation of one's being alienated by the other; will-to-power has its foundation in another project which is the assimilation of the in-itself-for-itself with the being-for-others. The aim of existential psychoanalysis would be the discovery of a first choice and concomitant situation. Such a system would exclude the use of a universal code of symbols after the Freudian pattern. Symbols would have to be interpreted according to each particular case and particular occasion.

3. Doing and having.

Although man's fundamental project has being *as an aim* (being in itself *and* for itself), *this project manifests itself mostly through the existential categories of* having *and* doing. *Having and doing are reducible to want of being: basically I make an object in order to have it. Having represents an extension of being. As such, the object I own is my self yet it is also in-itself. Possession is an attempt at realizing being-in-it-self-for-itself.*

Desire is lack of being; its ultimate aim is the realization of the ideal value of being-in-itself-for-itself. That realization is sought through the objects of the world. Although its pursuit is reducible to desire for being, it appears also under the forms of the creative and possessive urges. Doing, having, are the great categories of human existence:

One makes the object to keep up a certain relationship with it. This new relationship may be immediately reducible to "having." For instance, I cut a cane out of a tree branch (I "make" a cane with a branch) in order to *have* that cane. "Making" is reducible to a means of having. This is the most frequent case. But it may also happen that my activity does not appear immediately reducible. It may seem gratuitous as in the case of scientific research, of sport, of aesthetic creation. Yet, in these different cases, *making* is not irreducible either. If I create a picture, a drama, a melody, it is to be at the origin of a concrete existence. And this existence interests me only insofar as the bond of creation which I establish between it and myself gives me a particular right of property. The question is not that such a picture, the idea of which I have [in mind], should exist; it should also exist through me.[80]

My work is *mine,* because *I* have created it and because it has an existence *in itself.* It is one with my consciousness as representing an idea of mine, yet it is distinct from me as having the opacity of being-in-itself. It realizes the synthesis of the self and of the non-self.

The sense of appropriation extends to knowledge, to research, to sexual possession.

Knowledge is another form of appropriation. In knowledge, I am, at once, a creator, since an aspect of the world is revealed to me, and a possessor, since the aspect of the world I have revealed really *is,* outside of me. The truth I have discovered is independent from me and pursues an independent existence, as the work of art does. There is a sense of appropriation in research, as there is in discovery, as there is in parting the veils of mystery in any circumstances whatsoever. Knowledge is assimilation. It aims at identifying with the self something which remains the non-self. This is why sexual "possession" is referred to by the Bible as "knowledge." The known object is my thought as thing. There is truly no disinterested knowledge; *knowing* is one of the forms which *having* may take.

Play activities involve both doing and having. The world of games and sports is an artificial world governed by man-made laws. In that respect, it is both in-itself and for-itself. Appropriation plays a part in it inasmuch as it represents the acquisition of a fine body, mastery over the elements. This appropriation is merely a symbolic appropriation.

Play activity can be reduced to craving for being, both on the plane of doing and on the plane of having. A game is a form of activity the principles of which are established by man himself; to that extent, it represents an effort to live in an artificial world grounded in human consciousness, which is conformance to the ideal value of the in-itself-for-itself. Appropriation plays an important part in sports. Leaving aside the desire to own a fine body, which is part of our being-for-others, we seek in sports to assimilate our surroundings. To a skier, the snow represents pure exteriority, a sort of abstracted being-in-itself, yet solid and permanent. A child would try to appropriate this immaculate matter by fashioning a snow-man. The skier appropriates, through movement, the pure space suggested by the whiteness of the snow. Gliding adds a symbolic value to this movement. It is the image of an appropriation which does not interfere with the subject's transcendence. It is the opposite of being swamped down. A certain mode of being is revealed by skiing.

Political activities are also related to the quest of being through appropriation. The "haves" are simply striving to retain a world which they have made *their* world; the revolutionists want to create a new world the basis of which they will have established themselves.

Appropriation can exist only through the use I make of the object; it is purely symbolic.

Appropriation appears as a sort of continued creation. This is why having may be considered as an extension of being. Emerson illustrated how difficult it is to delineate the limits of the person: body, clothing, lodging—where is the line of demarcation to be drawn? Inasmuch as I appear to myself as creating objects by the mere rapport of appropriation, these objects are my self. Yet appropriation of an object can only

130

exist through the movement by which I transcend that object toward its use. If I think of an object without regard to its use, I see it as a thing in itself, and I am no longer anything but my being-for-itself. What possession tries to achieve is the symbolic realization of being-in-itself-for-itself. My possessions represent my transcendence, i.e., my subjectivity, and at the same time they confer on me that objectivity which I lack as pure consciousness. Through my possessions, I affirm to the other, and against the others, what I am. Yet, this relation remains as symbolical as the Freudian gratification of the libido. It cannot be realized, were it only because possession is an enterprise which death always causes to remain un-achieved. In other words: "You can't take it with you."

It is therefore frustrating and may lead to destruction which is a form of appropriation.

On becoming aware of the symbolic character of posses-sion, or if I am frustrated in my attempt to possess, I may be seized with the urge to destroy; for destruction is an attempt to realize appropriation. As I destroy, I impart to the being-in-itself the characters of my being-for-itself: its non-being and its translucidity. The object becomes mine as I have become the cause of its non-being. It has lost its irritating exteriority; it has assumed a past character. Moreover, I do not destroy for myself alone, but for the others as well. The satisfaction I experience in wearing out an object is of the same nature. We like the objects which bear the marks of the progressive de-struction resulting from the use we make of them. The more use we get out of them, the more it seems we have made them ours, the more we are attached to them, provided they still fulfil their functions. Giving an object away is also a form

131

of destruction. When I give away one of my possessions, I do away with it in a sense since I reduce it to being for me no more than an image; yet, at the same time, I oblige the new proprietor to bring it to life again as part of himself. The value I try to realize is my being-in-itself-for-itself-for-others.

When I appropriate an object, I am not merely trying to appropriate its being (in itself), I am trying to appropriate being as such and in general, because consciousness is lack of being. Through appropriation of an object we want to appropriate the whole of being, i.e., the world.

When I appropriate an object, my consciousness is attempting to appropriate more than its being in itself. What it tries to appropriate symbolically is being as such, the whole being in itself, i.e., the world. Each object possessed stands out on the background of the world it symbolizes. A yacht, for instance, is unthinkable outside of a certain way of life, and that certain way of life is a certain way of facing the world. When we smoke, as we reduce tobacco to smoke, on the rhythm of our respiration, the whole world of being is affected in its permanence and solidity; it is symbolically consumed; the taste of smoke, the warmth of the pipe-bowl are accessory details.

Thus, what we fundamentally desire to appropriate in an object is its being and it is the world. These two ends of appropriation are one in reality. I seek, behind the phenomenon, to possess the being of the phenomenon. But this being, very different, as we saw, from the phenomenon of being, is being-in-itself, and not merely the being of such or such a particular thing. It is not that there is here passage to the universal, but, rather, the being considered in its concrete bareness thereby becomes the being of totality. Thus the

132

rapport of possession clearly appears to us: to possess is to wish to possess the world through a particular object.[81]

To wish to possess an object, and through that object the world, is to aim at making of the being-for-itself the foundation of the concrete totality of being-in-itself, i.e., the world: "To-be-in-the-world is to project to possess the world, i.e., to apprehend the total world as what the for-itself lacks to become in-itself-for-itself." [82] The end of the being-for-itself is being-in-itself, but not the contingent in-itself which it negates. The being-for-itself wants to acquire as *consciousness* the infinite density of the in-itself. The desire for possession may now be defined in terms of desire for being:

> While the desire for being bears directly on the for-itself and projects to confer on it without intermediary the dignity of the in-itself-for-itself, the desire of having aims at the for-itself on, in, and through the world. It is through the appropriation of the world that the project of having aims at realizing the same value as the desire for being.[83]

Desire for being tends to confer being directly on the for-itself, desire for having intercalates the world between the for-itself and its being, establishing thereby the circuit of ipseity.

That object represents for us a certain manner of being which is the quality *of the object.*

Why do we choose to possess the world symbolically through a particular object rather than through another? What we aim at through a particular object is its being through a particular manner of being, which is its quality. Quality represents to us symbolically a certain manner of being; our very tastes symbolize our world outlook, our *Welt-*

133

anschauung. The predilection of each poet for a certain element: the geological element in Rimbaud, the fluidity of water in Poe, indicates, rather than a certain form of sexuality, the choice of a certain way of being.

The qualities *of things represent for us values or anti-values, according to our fundamental project in life.*

Symbolic appropriation of the qualities of things is the main clue to our life-project. The ultimate reality that existential psychoanalysis can reach, either directly or through appropriation, is neither a libido nor a will-to-power, but the choice of a certain way of being. In this latter case, things are chosen for the way in which they render being, and the way in which they render being is their quality. This quality may appear to us as value and also as an anti-value. According to our individual life-project, the viscous, for example, may exercise on us a certain fascination, or appear to us as repellent. The viscous may be evoked by a look, an attitude, a handshake. Common sense only sees in this evocation, a projection into certain human patterns of behavior, of my sensory experience of viscous matters. A purely material quality could not be projected into a psychic quality unless that material quality had first of all evoked an intrinsic quality similar to the psychic quality in question. Sartre's existential symbolism seems to agree with the Kantian definition of symbolism, according to which a true symbol is that object through which we see the same law operate as in the idea represented: e.g., the falling of leaves and old age. The viscous must appear immediately significant to us; otherwise we would not detect that significance in some human patterns of behavior. The

134

quality of viscosity, however, must have met with an appropriative project to acquire that significance for us. What is this particular quality? It is an ambiguous quality which at first evokes the fluidity of a liquid, flux and perpetual change, as in the Heraclitean philosophy of becoming; as its fluidity is slowed down by the liquid's tendency to turn to paste, it represents an incipient triumph of the solid over the liquid. Through the extraordinary description which Sartre gives us of viscosity, we understand the importance he attributes to this quality as anti-value; through it we understand that the for-itself, symbolized by the fluidity of viscosity, may be absorbed by the in-itself, symbolized by its tendency to congeal, in a sly, repulsive and fascinating sort of way. Through it, we understand that our past may slowly suck in our future. Our horror of viscous matters, glue, mire, quicksands, informs us of the constant danger our consciousness and our freedom run of being swamped, mired or absorbed by the contingency of the in-itself. Yet, even in this discovery, the for-itself remains free. It is the for-itself which brings this quality into being as a value, or rather as an anti-value representing something to be fled, the triumph of facticity over consciousness, the opposite of the in-itself-for-itself, such as Sartre found it represented by the skier's glide on the snow. This does not mean that viscosity in all forms is always an anti-value to all people; some people may not dislike being "swamped" by petty details which "allows them no time to think ahead." It simply means that viscosity has the same sense for everybody, although the evaluation of this sense varies according to the nature of each person's individual project. Such values, or anti-values, are formed early in life. Long before his sexuality is born, the child is revealed certain modes of being through the qualities of form or matter. The "anal tendencies" of the child do not spring from sexuality. They indicate his discovery of a mode of being. In itself, the hole is a symbol of a lack of being. It is a non-being to be filled with the being of one's flesh, so that there may be a plenitude of being. This is the true reason why the child presents the "anal" or "oral" tendencies detected by Freud. These tendencies may be related later with sexual tendencies but, on their first appearance, they certainly are pre-sexual.

Existential psychoanalysis should be able to detect our fundamental project through a study of our individual likes and dislikes.

Existential psychoanalysis may derive precious indications about the "human reality" in general from the behavior of the child. But its main concern would be to discover the individual project of each human being from its relation with various symbolical forms of being. Our likes and dislikes are revealing, even in the matter of food, since by absorbing it we assimilate its qualities: its taste, its texture, its color, its temperature. (A strangely accurate form of psychoanalysis has been developed lately in Switzerland out of the study of the subject's reaction to shades of various colors; it also bears on individual projects related with the problem of being in its most general aspect.) In his novels, Sartre made use of this existential symbolism. There is hardly any reaction of his characters to the form, color, and texture of things that is not related to the character's individual project. By way of illustration, we might mention here Mathieu's liking for green, for the sound of running water, for the fragrance of the pines; these qualities objectively represent the indecision, the fluidity, the expansion of a consciousness which wants to get out of itself as such: liberty for liberty's sake and without commitment. To him they are values. At various times, the contact of viscous matters makes him realize that his past is catching up with him, and that there cannot be liberty without commitment. Daniel's project, from the beginning, has been to seek his own objectivity in the look of others; he finds it finally in the look of God. The density of stone, opacity, darkness, black, remind him that his solution to the problem of being is to seek the darkness of being-in-itself.

Man's fundamental project, which is to ground being in consciousness, to realize the ideal value of being-in-itself and for-itself, i.e., the value which corresponds to the notion of God is doomed to failure.

These projects, however, and others, which we find embodied in various characters throughout Sartre's literary works, are mere variations, presumably failures, of the fundamental human project. Through the ontological reduction of psychoanalysis, every human project and every form of human behavior can be reduced to an attempt to realize being-in-itself-for-itself:

> Every human reality is a passion, inasmuch as it projects to lose itself to ground being and thereby constitute the In-itself which escapes contingency by being its own foundation, the *ens causa sui* which religions call God. Thus the passion of man is the opposite of Christ's, for man loses himself as man so that God may be born. But the idea of God is contradictory and we lose ourselves in vain; man is a useless passion.[84]

137

Conclusion

1. Metaphysical perspectives.

Consciousness is internal negation emanating from being. It constitutes an absolute of negation, an absolute without substance.

The for-itself is merely the negation of a particular being-in-itself. Having no autonomous substance outside of that negation, it has to seek its being in the in-itself. Consciousness is that *Other* described by Plato in *The Sophist,* which vanishes if you try to fix your attention upon him, and appears in the margin of things if you try to forget him. "Otherness is indeed internal negation and alone a consciousness can constitute itself as internal negation."[85] Yet, otherness emanates from being. Having no foundation of its own, it is relative to being. But in its rejection of its identity with being, it is an absolute, an absolute without substance.

138

At this point, the metaphysical question arises: why does the for-itself spring from the in-itself? Metaphysics, in its attempts to solve this problem, must take into account what ontology teaches us.

1) that if the in-itself had to ground itself, it could not even attempt it except by making itself consciousness, i.e., that the concept of *causa sui* entails in itself that of presence to self, i.e., of the nihilating decompression of being; 2) that consciousness is *in fact* the project to ground itself, i.e., of reaching the dignity of being-in-itself-for-itself, or in-itself-cause-of-itself.[86]

The teachings of ontology extend no further. As a matter of fact, they confront us with a contradiction:

To be the project of grounding itself, the in-itself should originally be presence to self, i.e., it should already be consciousness. Ontology will then limit itself to declare that *everything happens as if* the in-itself, in a project to ground itself, modified itself into the for-itself.[87]

It is now up to metaphysics to form hypotheses which will unify the data of ontology. It is up to the metaphysician to decide whether, before the appearance of consciousness, movement is not a first attempt of the in-itself to be its own foundation.

Metaphysics will have to form hypotheses concerning the totality of being in itself and for itself; it can neither constitute a dualism, since one is the internal negation of the other, nor a totality proper, since the in-itself-for-itself is an ideal value.

Metaphysics will have to consider a second problem. Do being-in-itself and being-for-itself constitute a dualism? It

139

would not seem so, since being-in-itself is connected to being-for-itself by an internal relation, and is inconceivable without being-in-itself. Do they constitute a totality? No doubt the for-itself needs the in-itself to exist, but the in-itself only needs the for-itself to assume phenomenal existence. As pure being, it does not need the for-itself. The totality in-itself-for-itself is conceivable only as a value: "Everything happens as if the world, man, and man-in-the-world, appeared in a state of disintegration in relation to an ideal synthesis. Not that the integration has ever taken place, but on the contrary, precisely because it is always indicated and always impossible." [88] We meet on the metaphysical plane the same sort of "detotalized totality" as on the plane of phenomenology. On the plane of pure reflection, the reflecting consciousness has to distinguish itself from the being reflected, as the reflected object has to distinguish itself from the reflecting consciousness. In the same way, the for-itself and the for-itself-for-others constitute a being in which each one confers otherness on the other by making itself other. If we consider now the relation between the totality of the in-itself and the for-itself, between consciousness and the world, we realize that the for-itself creates its otherness while the in-itself is not "other" in its being. It would seem then that I can grasp the totality of being in itself and myself, since I am at once *exhaustive consciousness* of being and consciousness of self. Metaphysics will have to choose whether to stop at the phenomenon with its two dimensions: for-itself and in-itself, or to retain the old dualism: "consciousness-being." If it adopts the new notion of the phenomenon as "disintegrated totality," it should be treated at once in terms of immanence and of transcendence: "Immanence will always be limited by the in-itself dimension of the

140

phenomenon, and transcendence by its for-itself dimension." [89]

Metaphysics will then have to consider the problem of action.

After deciding the question of the origin of the for-itself and of the nature of the world as phenomenon, metaphysics will be able to approach the problem of action. Action does not merely modify the phenomenal aspect of an object, since it can go as far as to negate the object altogether; the problem of action reveals to us a relation of being to being which is neither pure exteriority nor immanence, but refers us to the Gestaltist notion of form and background.

2. Moral perspectives.

Any system of ethics based on ontology should take into account the fact that man's ideal value is the realization of being-in-itself-for-itself. He should realize that he himself creates this value, as well as less fundamental values.

Ontology cannot formulate imperatives, but we can foresee a system of ethics resting on its data. It has revealed to us that value is a lack, and that all human projects point to the realization of being-in-itself-for-itself. Neither egoism, nor utility, nor interest, can explain human attitudes, since this realization transcends them all, and since one may say that "man makes himself man to be God," [90] i.e., his own cause. In such a system, the "spirit of seriousness" which consists in believing that values are transcendental data, and that the nature of things may furnish us rules of behavior, will have to be abandoned. Many men already know that the aim of their quest

141

is *being.* Many are reduced to despair for not being able to discover around them signs pointing to the ideal value of being-in-itself and for-itself. Man must realize that he is *the being through whom values exist.*

What will become of his ideal value, the *ens causa sui,* when man becomes conscious of it? Will he still retain it, and will it remain as the value that cannot be transcended? Will liberty adopt itself as the supreme value, being the source of all values? But what could be the meaning of a liberty that would itself constitute an end in itself? How could liberty, taking liberty for its end, escape the situation? All these questions, to be considered on the plane of pure reflection, were to be treated by Sartre in a separate treatise.

In existential ethics, the realization that my consciousness is an absolute would involve a sense of reciprocity. Every individual consciousness should, in principle, be considered as an end, not as a means to an end.

This treatise has not yet appeared, but Sartre has already given us a few hints about the general principles on which his ethical system would rest. These were further developed and illustrated in such plays as *Huis-clos* and *Les Mouches.* They seem to fit in with the system delineated by Sartre's disciple, Simone de Beauvoir, in *Pour une morale de l'ambiguïté,* and we may take for granted that the disciple expresses the idea of the master when she states that, each consciousness being an absolute, "the other steals the world from me every instant," [91] and that it is quite true as Hegel claims that "each consciousness pursues the death of the other";[92] even though, on the other hand, each consciousness finds its solidarity with

142

the others in the very act by which it distinguishes itself from them: "Each man needs the liberty of others, and, in a sense, he always wants it, were he even a tyrant; he simply fails to assume in good faith the consequences of such a want."[93] Existential ethics would make the liberty of man the end of all our actions. Each consciousness, being an absolute, would have to be treated as an end and not as a means to an end.

The fact that this ideal is unattainable does not do away with our responsibility.

Obviously, such an ideal is unattainable since the pursuit of man's liberty may in some cases—for instance, in a war of liberation—entail the sacrifices of certain individuals or even of a whole generation. In existential ethics, however, no situation would ever allow the responsible person to delegate his responsibility to divine or "historical" powers. As in Huxley, so in Simone de Beauvoir and in Sartre, ends and means constitute a single movement and the means condition the ends. Such a conclusion leaves us indeed with a certain impression of ambiguity.

Sartre's political philosophy illustrates these principles.

One principle, however, seems to emerge plainly from the general conception of existential ethics in both Simone de Beauvoir and Sartre: the principle of reciprocity. Insofar as my consciousness appears to me as an absolute, and basically constitutes my center of reference, I must realize that the other's consciousness is also an absolute for him. This principle is the basis of Sartre's political philosophy, which it may not be inopportune to recall at this point.

3. The social problem.

Capitalism exploits the idealist myth; communism, the materialist myth: Sartre rejects both.

According to Sartre, the present world situation can be defined as the struggle between Capitalism and Communism. Capitalism, states Sartre somewhat sweepingly, exploits the idealist myth and Communism the materialist myth. Following the same line as in his philosophy, Sartre rejects both. Capitalism means more or less the status quo. It allows the individual to pass from one class to the other, but it maintains the exploitation of the laboring class by the governing class. Yet the liberty which the possessing class enjoys is a somewhat barren kind of contemplative liberty, since it is condemned by its very nature to remain conservative. The liberty left to the laboring classes is that of choosing its masters. Yet, if it does not constitute real democracy, it is, at least, excellent democratic education.

Communism is a double imposture. As materialism, it reduces the movements of the mind to those of matter, yet claims for itself the privilege of contemplating the universe, thereby substituting itself, as pure objectifying look, for the God which it denies.

As to Communism, or dialectical materialism, it is an obvious imposture for the following reasons: Materialism, which denies the existence of God and transcendental finality, reduces the movements of the mind to those of matter, and eliminates subjectivity by reducing the world, with man in it, to a system of objects bound by universal connections.

144

Materialism is really a metaphysical system, yet Marxists refuse to defend their position on metaphysical grounds, and take refuge in a new kind of positivism. Their materialism, they say, is the expression of a progressive discovery of the interaction of the world, a discovery which is not passive but implies the activity of the discoverer. Thus the materialist denies subjectivity, becomes himself an object among others, the matter for scientific knowledge. But once he has suppressed subjectivity, instead of seeing himself as a thing among things, he starts considering himself as a pure objective look and claims to contemplate the world as it is. Having gone beyond all subjectivity and assimilated himself to pure objective truth, he wanders in a world of objects inhabited by man-objects. He abandons science together with subjectivity, steps out of humanity, and substitutes himself for God, whom he denies, to contemplate the spectacle of the universe. Back from his trip, he tells us that everything that is real is rational, which might make sense coming from a Kantian, but makes none coming from a materialist. If reason is governed from outside, how can it remain reason? "Consciousness," says Lenin, "is only the reflection of being, approximately exact in the best cases." But who will determine what the best cases are without idealist criteria or values? In the end, the materialist destroys his metaphysics with his positivism, his positivism with his rationalism.

Opposition makes sense in Hegel's totality of Mind, but not in a materialist philosophy.

That is not all; Marxism is *dialectical* materialism. These two terms, says Sartre, cannot be reconciled. Dialectics can

145

function only within a totality like Hegel's totality of Mind. Matter is a sum, not a totality. (Even Einstein's relationships remain quantitative and external.) Matter is expressed by quantity and the scientific method is expressed by quantitative measurements. There can be no opposition in matter. Matter is inert, its energy comes from without. Still less can there be a synthesis within matter in the Hegelian sense.

Communism may be successful, but only for the party in power.

The cause of materialism remains then associated with practical considerations. This is obvious in the attempts made by Marxists to study social "superstructures." These are, for the Marxists, the reflections of the systems of production. The conditions of material life in society, says Stalin, determine its ideas, its theories, its political opinions, its political institutions; but he also states that "new ideas are brought about by new tasks to be accomplished." How can we, says Sartre, believe both affirmations? Is the idea determined by the social conditions, or is it brought about, or suggested, by new tasks to be accomplished? The last statement implies finality. Belief in certain ideas is necessary to solve certain problems perhaps —and there is no doubt that there is a connection between the situation of an oppressed class and the materialistic expression of that situation; but we cannot conclude that materialism is a philosophy, still less that it is the truth. Materialists will finally argue that, whether it is the truth or not, it has been successful; but, concludes Sartre, it has been successful only with the party in power which has become the sole proprietor of the state.

146

Sartre's own "Rally" would be democratic insofar as democracy involves recognition of the other's liberty. It would be revolutionary inasmuch as liberty has to be conquered from a given situation.

We recognize in this criticism of idealism and of materialism in politics the general outline of Sartre's philosophy. Out of this philosophy he has evolved the program which he advocates: a rally for revolutionary Democracy. There must be a rally because there is no room for a new party and because parties belong to the past anyway. This rally would be made up of all people dissatisfied with existing parties. It should be democratic because men can insure their freedom only by accepting the fact that they need the freedom of others as foundation for their own. It must be revolutionary because you have to conquer your own liberty in order to experience freedom. The revolution must come from the oppressed since they will experience liberty only in action. They must recognize the elements which have given rise to the materialistic outlook since, after all, work, fatigue and hunger are pressing realities, but this recognition can only emerge in the light of a situation to be transcended toward an entirely new situation. Instead of trying to generalize, under the color of universal materialism, the conditions from which they suffer, so that the oppressors may in their turn feel the pressure of events, they should recognize that in order to be free, one has to have his own freedom recognized by other free beings.

A plurality of free consciousnesses is possible on the plane of doing, *within a common transcendence. Mastery of the universe might provide a common aim, and a common transcendence, on the plane of work.*

147

One might, at this point, wonder what became of Sartre's pessimism, how he can now admit that a free consciousness may recognize another free consciousness, that a free subject can recognize anything except objects. But the sort of recognition which he now recommends is merely the experience of common transcendence which he has already described in *L'Être et le néant;* it takes place on the plane of doing, not on the plane of being. The revolutionist sees human relations from the point of view of work, and work implies as an end common to all men the mastery of the universe. Thus, in this clarified conception of Heidegger's *Mitsein,* as a kind of team spirit, a multiplicity of subjects can coexist thanks to a common object to be acted upon: the universe.

Sartre's projected Rally was to allow a constant interchange of views between the top and the bottom of the structure.

The Rally Sartre envisaged was to work partly through unions and partly through sections representing local interests. Collaboration between the basis and the top of the Rally's structure was to become a permanent element in its operation and, in time, the basis was to discover that each of its particular problems could be solved only as part of a general problem. According to him, this double movement is essential in all democracies and is the mark of real emancipation.[94]

Having failed to organize his Rally, Sartre seems to have drawn closer to Marxism, without disavowing his very lucid criticism of the inconsistencies within that system.[95] His view seems to be that Marxism raised the questions most relevant to the general situation of our modern society. Even though they were formulated according to a faulty method of knowledge and solved in the wrong way, so long as these questions are not practically solved Marxism will remain a most living force.

Our purpose however, was to present in this study, not Sartre's own ambiguous answers to the challenge of Marxism, but the questions raised by his philosophy of negativity, in such a way as to make it easier for the reader to formulate his answer to them.

Notes

Introduction

1. *The Republic of Silence,* tr. by A. J. Liebling. Harcourt, Brace, 1947.

2. So he is called by F. H. Heinemann in *Existentialism and the Modern Predicament.* Harper Torchbooks, 1958.

3. Iris Murdoch, *Sartre, Romantic Rationalist.* New Haven, Yale Univ. Press, 1953.

4. By Hazel A. Barnes in *The Literature of Possibility.* Lincoln, Univ. of Nebraska Press, 1959.

5. By James Collins in *The Existentialists, A Critical Study.* Chicago, Henry Regnery, 1952.

TEXT

The references are to Jean-Paul Sartre's *L'Être et le néant* (Paris, Gallimard, 1943), which will be cited as EN. Translations are by the author.

1. EN, p. 17.
2. EN, p. 18.
3. EN, p. 19.
4. EN, p. 18.
5. EN, p. 23.
6. EN, p. 23.
7. EN, p. 27.

8. EN, p. 28.
9. EN, p. 29.
10. EN, p. 34.
11. EN, p. 44.
12. EN, p. 42.
13. EN, p. 44.
14. EN, pp. 46, 47.

NOTES

15. EN, pp. 60, 61.
16. EN, p. 61.
17. EN, p. 62.
18. EN, p. 64.
19. EN, p. 65.
20. EN, p. 65.
21. EN, pp. 65, 66.
22. EN, p. 72.
23. EN, p. 72.
24. EN, p. 72.
25. EN, p. 81.
26. EN, p. 82.
27. EN, p. 83.
28. EN, p. 92.
29. EN, p. 92.
30. EN, p.116.
31. EN, p. 119.
32. EN, pp. 119, 120.
33. EN, p. 122.
34. EN, p. 124.
35. EN, p. 126.
36. EN, p. 127.
37. EN, p. 140.
38. EN, p. 140.
39. EN, p. 143.
40. EN, p. 146.
41. EN, p. 149.
42. EN, p. 150.
43. EN, p. 169.
44. EN, p. 172.
45. EN, p. 195.
46. EN, pp. 195, 196.
47. EN, p. 205.
48. EN, p. 231.
49. EN, p. 235.
50. EN, p. 241.
51. EN, p. 251.
52. EN, p. 253.
53. EN, p. 270.
54. EN, p. 285.
55. EN, p. 300.

56. EN, p. 355-356.
57. EN, p. 358.
58. EN, p. 361.
59. EN, p. 362.
60. EN, p. 363.
61. EN, *Ibid*.
62. EN, p. 430.
63. EN, p. 441.
64. EN, p. 444.
65. EN, p. 449.
66. EN, p. 460.
67. EN, p. 478.
68. EN, p. 479.
69. EN, p. 481.
70. EN, p. 493.
71. EN, pp. 497-498.
72. EN, p. 498.
73. EN, p. 515.
74. EN, p. 555.
75. EN, p. 597.
76. EN, p. 599.
77. EN, p. 653.
78. EN, p. 653.
79. EN, pp. 653-654.
80. EN, p. 665.
81. EN, p. 687.
82. EN, p. 688.
83. EN, p. 689.
84. EN, p. 708.
85. EN, p. 712.
86. EN, p. 715.
87. EN, p. 715.
88. EN, p. 717.
89. EN, p. 719.
90. EN, p. 720.
91. Simone de Beauvoir, *Pour une morale de l'ambiguïté,* Paris, Gallimard, 1947, p. 99.
92. *Ibid*.
93. Simone de Beauvoir, *op. cit.,* p. 100.

151

94. The political views condensed above are from *Situations,* III, Paris, Gallimard, 1949. *"Matérialisme et révolution,"* pp. 135-225. Sartre's criticism of Communism applies mostly to Marxism as practiced in Russia in 1949 but also bears on Marx's philosophical approach.

95. This criticism is reproduced almost verbatim in *Critique de la raison dialectique,* Paris, Gallimard, 1960, pp. 30-31.

Index

Aquinas, Thomas: his tradition, xiv

Aristotle: and christianity, xiv

Atheism: defined by Marcel, xxiv; defined by Berdyaev, xxv; Sartre's atheism, xxxix, xl

Augustine: and existentialism, xiv-xv

Beauvoir, S. de: on Sartre, xxxi, xxxii, xxxiii, on ethics, 143

Behaviorism: Sartre's criticism, 76

Berdyaev: and existentialism, xxiv-xxvi; on non-being, xxxiv

Bergson: and existentialism, xx-xxi; source of Marcel, xxiv; source of Berdyaev, xxiv; compared with Husserl, xxvii; on non-being, xxxiv, 12-13; his notion of liberty criticized by Sartre, 21; his "duration" criticized by Sartre, 44, 82; his *"élan vital,"* 49; "pure memory," 115

Berkeley: *esse est percipi*, 3

Buber: and existentialism, xxi-xxii; compared with Marcel, xxiii, xxiv

Calvin: in Augustine's tradition, xiv

Camus: and the school of commitment, xxxi

Christian Science: and psychoanalysis, 25

Descartes: Augustine's influence on, xiv; and existentialism, xv-xvi; his *cogito* criticized by Marcel, xxiii, by Husserl, xxvi, by Sartre, 6; his "thinking substance" rejected by Sartre, 6; his argumentation compared with Sartre's, 8; Cartesian doubt and Husserl's "bracketing," 9; liberty, 16; the idea of perfection, 29

Freud: Sartre's criticism of his subconscious, 22-23; and psychoanalysis, 25; Sartre rejects his theory, 108; Sartre adopts his method, 126; symbolic gratification, 131; Sartre rejects Freudian sexuality, 136

Gestalt: form and background, 51; form, 76

Gnostics: source of Berdyaev, xxiv

Hegel: and existentialism, xiv; negativity, xvii, 105, 106; his influence on Heidegger's late works, xxx; on non-being, xxxiv; determination as negation, 12; on essence, 20; on consciousness, 47; point of view of the totality criticized by Kierkegaard, xvii, commented on by

The manuscript was edited by Ita Kanter. The book was designed by Richard Kinney and Richard Berube. The text type face is Linotype Granjon, designed in 1924 by George W. Jones, based on a face originally cut by Claude Garamond in the 16th Century. The display face is Weiss designed by E. R. Weiss and cut by Bauer in 1926.

This book is printed on Warren's 1854 Text regular finish paper. The soft cover edition of this book is bound in Warren's Cameo Brilliant Cover and the hard cover edition is bound in Joanna Mills Natulin. This book was manufactured in the United States of America.